# MISSION: POSSIBLE

## A decade of living dangerously

**by ASH DYKES**

Published in 2017
by Eye Books
29A Barrow Street
Much Wenlock
Shropshire
TF13 6EN
www.eye-books.com

ISBN: 978-1-78563-046-0

British Library Cataloguing in Publication Data
A catalogue record for this book is available from the British Library

Printed by CPI Group (UK) Ltd, Croydon CR0 4YY

# CONTENTS

**(Inset: PHOTO ALBUM)**

# PROLOGUE: Gobi Desert, 2014

Sharp stones on the hard, sandy ground where I lay poked like nails into my back. Just a few inches above me was my steel trailer with my tent and other kit loaded on top, and I tried to avoid touching the hot metal. I'd shuffled underneath it to shield my upper body from the burning sun, but my legs stuck out the end and felt as if they were melting. I imagined how I would look if there were anyone around to see me, but there wasn't anyone for miles: in my mind's eye, the camera panned out into the sky over an empty expanse of bright pale desert until I was an insignificant speck, a dot gradually fading from view.

I put the water bottle to my blistered lips. I'd been daydreaming of cold, clear, fresh water, babbling brooks, gushing taps – but the dregs left in the bottle were as hot as tea and tasted sour. The heat was relentless – it must have been over 40°C – and I'd been trekking since morning, weak and semi-delirious, my eyes tired from searching the horizon for signs of a settlement. By this time I had been walking for 43 days through the Gobi; dragging the 18-stone trailer through sand had been tough from the beginning, but now every step was demanding. The last food I'd eaten hadn't spent much time in my system, and my body was running on empty. My mind had been wandering as my body struggled on.

I had ventured into the Gobi Desert, known as the harshest desert in the world, earlier than anticipated, taking a route without confirmed water sources. Although I'd made it through that section I'd had to ration my water for a few weeks and the dehydration had been getting worse without my feeling any symptoms. Now, in the hottest and worst part of my route through the desert, where there were no water points for several days at a time, it had all hit me and I was suffering the consequences in the most severe way. I remembered the eerie skeletons of camels I'd walked past in the middle of nowhere. The thought entered my head, a sudden clear thought emerging from the fog, that this could be my impossible day: the day I might not succeed, the day my expedition would fail… the day I could die.

People had said it was impossible to cross the country this way, walking all the way alone through mountains and desert and steppe… No-one had done it before. It just wasn't possible, they said. Were they right?

*No.* If I could just make it 100 more metres, I could rest again, and if I could keep going like this, I would make it to a settlement, however long it took, and someone would give me water. I had to believe it. Somehow the need to prove people wrong, to prove that I could do it – and perhaps just the will to live – galvanised me to pull myself up. My muscles ached but I gritted my teeth against the pain, cursing. *Must continue*, I said to myself, *no matter what.* Determined to keep pushing on, I broke the goal down into small steps. Step by step.

It was resilience and mental strength, I believe, that got me through these days, making it all possible again. It was also thanks to my previous experience. I don't know if I'd have been able to walk across Mongolia if I hadn't done everything that came before. Every step of the journey of the previous years had built up to a powerful force that helped me survive.

Crossing Mongolia solo and unsupported, becoming the first person known to have done so, was my first big expedition, which I completed at the age of 23. Several years before, I'd decided I wanted to go into the unknown, throw myself far out of my comfort zone, push my personal limits, experience as much as I could and see what was possible. My insatiable appetite to explore and to challenge myself was there already. To me, that was truly living. But growing up on an ordinary street in an ordinary town in North Wales, it had felt like a crazy idea to make such a huge dream happen.

# Part One:
# GETTING STARTED

# 1: Making a mind map and the money to set out

It was still dark when my alarm went off: 4am. I silenced it quickly, wishing I could ignore it – but across the gloom of my bedroom I could see the world map, and knew why I was doing this. I braced myself for the cold as I flung off the bedcovers, grabbed my backpack and crept into the hallway, avoiding the creaky floorboard, trying not to wake Brodey. Within five minutes I was opening the back door and jumping on my bike. The wind blew off the Irish Sea and rain slapped me in the face. Oh, the joys of winter on the coast of North Wales! The only solution was to cycle as fast as possible, get the heart going and warm up. And remember all the money I was saving by not having a car.

Eight miles later I skidded into the car park at Llandudno swimming baths, locked up the bike and made my way into the showers, turning on the lights and pulling everything I needed out of my bag. The hot water felt good and I could hear others arriving for the early shift. I dressed in the standard polo shirt and shorts, gave Mat a high-five as I passed him in the corridor, and assumed my position at the side of the pool, wrinkling my nose at that familiar smell of chlorine and bodies, ready for a mind-numbing morning of watching the regulars swim up and down. Up and down. Up and down.

Routine and repetition were things I hated and fought against. But I was an 18-year-old on a mission. I had a goal. I had planning to do when I got back home – that's why I opted for those five-until-two shifts, so I'd have the afternoon to myself. This was all about building up the money and making plans in my free time. I wanted to believe I was on my way to being an adventurer, but they don't tend to offer that as a career choice at your average comprehensive school in a small town like Old Colwyn, so I was figuring out the route myself.

At school I'd always had a bit too much fun, to the annoyance of some teachers, enjoying it not for the lessons but the social life. I was one of the smallest kids but one of the loudest and cockiest, and in the classroom I tended to mess about, easily distracted, not paying attention to subjects I wasn't interested in. I was your typical average boy, looking to have a good time and enjoy the here and now.

I wasn't a particularly naughty kid but I did take risks. Once I was racing down the street on my bike and a car pulled out and knocked me down. On another occasion, I fell off somehow and broke my collar bone, and I hated wearing a helmet because it made me look silly. One time I was doing a stunt and fell on my face. I could feel my tooth was chipped. I got up fast and said to my friend: 'Don't tell my mum! She can't find out!'

He laughed and said, 'You got no choice, she's going to find out

– look at your face!'

I looked in a car's wing mirror and saw my face all banged up, blood all over the place.

Weekends and holidays were all about playing football or tennis, mountain biking and camping out in the countryside close to home: the mountains of Snowdonia National Park were a stone's throw away, there were woods on the hills and a huge stretch of beach. I loved my sports; I would try anything and everything, and was something of a fitness fanatic, running for Wales in the cross-country team. My dad had bought a multi-gym and a treadmill for our house when I was 14, and I got into training more heavily – I learned from research and reading on the internet, using bodyweight rather than weights.

When I was doing my Duke of Edinburgh Award at school, we had to volunteer at the fire service. There must have been about 25 of us lads, and the firemen set out a challenge with push-ups, pull-ups, sit-ups and so on, with a competition to see who could do the most in a set time. I definitely wasn't the biggest of the group, but my competitive streak came out, adrenaline kicking me into high gear, and I put everything I had into it. When the whistle went, I was panting and red-faced, bent over to catch my breath, my pulse racing. We stood in line, waiting for the results. "In first place… Ash Dykes!" It's amazing what a competition can do to your performance.

My parents were also into exercise and outdoor activities, so it was part of life from when I was young. I remember jogging alongside my dad at the age of 11, and I had so much energy, I was punching leaves, talking away as we went while he was exhausted doing our five-mile jog up and down hilly terrain. I also went up Snowdon with my dad; we intended to walk but ended up jogging to the top and running back down. With my elder sister Tash, we went abroad a few times on family holidays, trips to Lanzarote, to America, to Canada, and were never the types to lounge around the swimming pool for a whole week, always renting a car to go out and see the place or engaging in different activities. We did a winter activity holiday in Lapland – skiing, snowmobiling, snowboarding, husky and reindeer rides. They were quite fun and packed-out holidays. I loved the adrenaline stuff – in America, we'd go to the theme parks and I was always on the rollercoasters.

After I finished my GCSEs at school, I didn't know what I wanted to do next. My parents never went in for the old-fashioned lines "you *must* do this and you *must* do that". They were pretty cool parents and gave me freedom, but also the strictness and guidance I needed not to go off in the wrong direction. So they insisted that I go on to further education, but I was given a choice: to stay on for A-levels or head to college. The obvious answer for me was college, and I found a two-year course for a BTEC National Diploma in Outdoor Education, which offered plenty of hands-on experience away from the books.

I applied and got an interview – but after I completed my exams, I found I didn't have the grades to get on the course. The head tutor said he noticed I'd had a lot of outdoors experience for someone so young, and that he'd take a risk and go with experience over qualifications just this once. I was over the moon, and wasn't going to let him down. The course included lots of theory, but it was a subject I was truly interested in, with a good amount of outdoor practical work – rock climbing, winter mountaineering, avalanche awareness, kayaking and canoeing – and I threw myself into every activity.

A lot of people on the course had top-end waterproof gear, and when they saw me turn up in an Adidas "drizzleproof" jacket they all told me, "You're going to suffer wearing that kit – that's for the football pitch, not the mountains and definitely not for winter!" I took it as a challenge to prove them wrong. "It's all in the mind," I said, laughing. Later, when I was sodden wet and shivering with cold, I put on a brave face as if I was absolutely fine, warm and dry... I think they believed me. And it all brought out the adventurous spirit in me even more.

As the first year drew to an end, everyone started looking at what they would do next. It was decision time again. Some wanted to join the RAF or the Army, some wanted to continue to university so they could teach. I still wasn't completely sure what I wanted – but I was finished with the classroom and had no desire to fit into a conventional life with the grind of nine-to-five work, living for the weekends and just getting by until you die. This life is so short, I felt, even at the age of 17; why not experience as much as possible in the time gifted to you? I had a desire to be doing something. Living shouldn't be just existing. The SAS had always sounded exciting but I believed I could find tough challenges myself. I wanted something exhilarating that would keep me on the knife-edge of life.

I was a dreamer, I suppose; evenings would find me mesmerised by documentaries about wildlife and remote tribes in faraway places. There was a huge world out there with so much to discover and I knew so little. I had a fantasy of taking on adventures abroad, simply setting off to explore different countries, learning the local way of life, challenging myself on big, extreme expeditions where I would face all sorts of dangers and difficulties. I imagined developing myself this way, and figured that throwing myself out into the world would make me stronger and wiser as a person.

I'm a big believer in experience. I will always have time to listen to someone who has been there and done it. People who achieved great things against all odds have always been an inspiration to me, the believers and achievers in all walks of life, athletes and other individuals who rose to the top of their game in whatever field.

Sport did have its buzz – training hard always seemed to reset my mind to make me believe anything was possible – but travelling was far more of a thrill for me. There'd be no restrictions, no coach to tell me what to do and what not to do: I'd be leading myself. The idea of all that freedom and variety, rather than restriction and repetition, excited me. When you're travelling, every path is different. There would be incredible times, scary and possibly life-threatening times; I felt ready for it – and even if I wasn't, I felt that learning through experience and mistakes was the best way to develop. You try not to make the same mistake twice – what counts is to learn from it. As an athlete, to a certain extent you're in your comfort zone – your diet is looked after, your training regime is looked after – and I loved the idea of taking care of absolutely everything, being in charge and having to learn, extensively developing myself.

It sounds glamorous and bold, but it also seemed close

to impossible. I was halfway through a college course, I was spending money on a car that I'd just modified with a body kit, sound system and alloy wheels that I'd bought second hand from eBay – it was just a phase but an expensive one – and I was still working as a waiter making £3-£4 an hour. At that rate there was no way I'd be able to save enough money to get started and turn my dreams into reality. There were too many things that would have to change to make it happen. It was daft, unfeasible. And yet the more I thought about it, the more I wanted it. One day at the end of the college year, before I headed to work, I told my dad what I was planning.

My dad's a cool guy; more like a big brother, as we get on so well and laugh so hard with one another. He was instantly hooked and loved the idea. We immediately went outside with a pen and paper. It was a hot summer's day, and my brother Brodey, then aged three, was sitting in the shade, playing on the grass, as my mum did a bit of gardening. My dad and I sat on deck chairs and bounced ideas back and forth, hatching a plan together.

I knew my parents weren't the types to make it easy or hand me loads of money. In any case, they didn't have loads of money to give. While I was growing up, Dad did a range of jobs from financial advisor and mortgage consultant to store manager. My mum worked part-time for the NHS, as a medicine dispenser at a doctor's surgery – it was handy to have a first aid provider in the family – and did voluntary work for the NSPCC's Childline. They were already working hard and had Brodey to take care of, as well as me and my sister Tash, who was at Bangor university in North Wales studying criminology.

My parents were there when I needed them, but they didn't want me to become too dependent, where I couldn't do stuff for myself; they tried to raise me to sort my own problems out. They were 100 per cent supportive, always there to listen, help direct and give guidance, but they instilled in me that feeling that if something needs to be done, you do it yourself – nobody's going to hand it to you on a plate.

And so Dad and I sat there and, with the ideas flowing, sketched out a mind map. It was basically a spider diagram on a plain piece of paper: "World Travels" written in the middle, and scattered all around it were lines shooting off in all directions. It was as if those lines were the paths leading to the goal, and in the little bubbles I wrote all the stuff I wanted, from destinations to duration, and everything I'd have to plan, from visas to vaccinations.

I broke the money concept down into how many hours I could work a day, from that how much I could save per month and from that, what dates I could think about leaving. I wrote "qualification to take abroad" – perhaps I could earn an income whilst I was travelling.

Later, I stuck it to my bedroom wall. I also pinned up a big map of the world, and in the middle I placed a badge that a friend had given me with the SAS motto, "Who Dares Wins".

I decided I needed about £10–12,000 to go off travelling for a good length of time. Instead of aiming for that huge end target, if I could just lay this goal out and break it down into sections, and take it step by step, each step would get me closer to the end goal. I was spending a lot of money on my car – tax, MOT, petrol – so I made the decision to sell it, buy myself a push bike and start cycling. Step one: tick!

Since working as a waiter for a few pounds an hour wasn't going to get me far, I decided to take my lifeguard qualification over the summer holidays before the second year of college, to open up the possibility of saving more. I'd been told it was a well-paid job for a teenager. Once I passed, I found work at Llandudno swimming centre just a few days after my 18th birthday, and said yes to every shift that was offered.

I was soon working long hours, about 200–240 a month, cycling to work in the early hours of the morning after creeping out of the house in the dark so I didn't wake up my little brother, as then he'd wake my parents. The work of watching people swim up and down bored me to tears, but I kept my eye on the target. I held back on nights out, as that was just a way of spending the money I needed for travel. I was pretty strict and disciplined with myself, and instead of going out with mates to the pub, I'd stay at home planning my travels and training.

Gradually, over that summer, my bedroom wall filled up not only with the mind map and the world map but also with pictures of places I wanted to go to, and inspirational quotes. I was interested in concepts like The Law of Attraction, where we attract into our lives whatever we focus on, visualizing a picture of what we want our life to be and thinking positive rather than negative thoughts. I wanted to push myself, and find out what was possible.

My friends didn't always get it. One of my best friends had posters on his wall of *The Simpsons* and wrestling champions – we were completely different, but maybe that's why we got on so well. When I told him I wanted to walk the Great Wall of China one day, he sort of scratched his head and said, "And then what – what will you do after, when you get back?" He couldn't see that as a goal in itself, because he wanted a life of comforts and luxuries – which is fair enough, but it wasn't what I wanted. I was inspired by something different.

The gang who worked with me lifeguarding were good fun, and I started to spend more time with them – partly because I almost lived there. After working the morning shift, I'd cycle home and often get a call to go back in – they knew I wanted the hours, because I was so determined to raise as much money as possible. I'd cycle all the way back for another shift. We'd have a laugh, pushing each other in the pool, often getting up to silly stuff to get through the day.

It was that kind of a day when I first got chatting to Mat, who was the second lifeguard on duty with me. It was a quiet afternoon and we'd both been watching one single swimmer in her swimming cap lap the pool, up and down, up and down… I started having rant about the latest Health and Safety regulation. We'd just been informed by the management, via a notice on the board in the staff room, that we were no longer allowed to hand out the swimming floats to children.

"Can you believe it? Because if a kid puts the float underwater it might pop out and hit them in the face. They might get hurt – by a polystyrene float! I tell you I can't stand it, man – it might be safe but it's not healthy…"

Mat stared at me ranting away, then without saying a thing he bopped himself on the nose with a float and rolled his eyes, pretending to go dizzy, exaggerating every aspect possible. We both burst out laughing.

"I mean, there shouldn't be a sign on a step saying 'Mind the step'. You've got eyes: you should use your eyes. You've got to make mistakes to learn."

Seriously, I hated all those rules, and I hated the Health and Safety regulations even more when they said we weren't allowed to work as many shifts, or lark about and chuck our colleagues in the pool. But in the meantime, I became friends with Mat. He was a year older than me, and had been living next door to me during the last year of high school, but because he was in the year above, I never really spoke to him. He was quite shy and quiet; a bit of a dark horse. I didn't know much about him.

He had only popped up on the radar after a very unfortunate car accident when he was 18. He had been the sole survivor; his two friends in the same car had died, as did the driver in the other car involved. Mat had been in the back seat and it had taken the fire service a long time to open up the car to rescue him; he was lucky to get away with just a broken leg. He was off work for quite some time. We'd all been shocked by the incident.

As we got talking, he asked me about the outdoor course I was doing. I told him all about it and he asked:

"So why don't you want to be an outdoor instructor?"

That was opening the floodgates. I blurted out some of the wild ideas I had for going travelling. My enthusiasm must have rubbed off on him as he admitted that he too loved the thought of just taking off to explore. In fact, he said, he wouldn't mind coming along. This threw me somewhat as I had a loose arrangement to go with another friend, and at that stage I barely knew Mat. I didn't know if we'd get along. But it didn't take long to figure out that I clicked with him and that this idea of taking on mad adventures was something he really wanted too.

He explained that the accident had changed his perspective on life, as he realised how fast it could be taken. It was this that made him decide he wanted to go and truly live his life, having been granted this second chance. He realised just how precious life is and how important is it to do the things that make you feel alive, things that you appreciate.

We started meeting regularly to talk through ideas and plans. We got excited looking through magazines and thinking about different places that we could go to, things we could do – taking on the world's highest bungee jump, learning how to surf, trying different martial arts, learning survival from tribal communities. One of us would come up with an idea and there was never any, "Nah, I don't like the sound of that…" It was always, "Yeah, love it!" So I knew he'd be a great travelling companion.

It became our life and we were obsessed by it all, putting in the hard work and dedication, but at the same time having a great laugh during the process, and often playing pranks on one another. One day we were both cycling back from work against the wind and came to a railing that split the path. I said to Mat, "You take the left path, I'll take the right." I thought he'd know what I was up to, but I got him. He agreed and followed the path downhill, and I was crying with laughter as I set off on the other path, knowing he'd ended up at the bottom of a long staircase. He'd be laughing and shouting at me through the wind as he carried his bike up the steps. It was the continual banter that formed our bond.

Mat was focused too and once he saw all the training I was doing – jogging, cycling, boxing, step and/or hill sprints, as well as body weight exercises like push-ups, pull-ups, sit-ups – he also wanted to push himself to train and get physically ready. He had to be careful at first about getting into training, but I helped him along, going for short jogs with him and building up to more until he said he felt better than ever before, physically and mentally. Soon we were both inspired and believed that we could do whatever we wanted if we dedicated ourselves to it.

Mat's parents had been quite wary of the idea of him taking off to the other side of the world – and rightly so, after he'd been so lucky to survive his accident. They're a different generation to mine, so the plan came as a bit of a shock and Mat had to ease them into it, gradually extending the duration of the travel bit by bit. As soon as they realised this was what he truly wanted, they went ahead and supported the idea.

As for my parents, my dad had been involved in my planning and preparation from the start so he understood that I was going about things in the proper way. Mum was more worried at first. But my mum and I have a very strong connection; she'd always been there to talk things through, keeping me level-headed. Mum was part of everything, she'd got used to the idea and was excited and enthusiastic for me too. Mat and I had plans to be away for the next four years, travelling and working, though we could come back home from time to time.

Throughout that year Mat and I worked every shift possible, and would try to get on the same shift to talk things over, keeping each other on track and motivated with ideas. We formed a solid bond. It was then that I raised the notion that instead of coming back after the money ran out, we could find work abroad. There are so many opportunities in the world and it's not all about this little island where we were born. We looked at becoming ski instructors at first, but the set-up costs were expensive, so then we thought about becoming scuba diving instructors. Since 75 percent of the world is water and the largest populations live on the coast, if we learned how to scuba dive we could find work while we travelled – in Asia, Australia, wherever.

We found a training centre based in Chester in England, not too far from us, where we could gain our Open Water, Advanced and Rescue Diver certificates– the first three qualifications. After that you need to start logging dives in order to take your Dive Master qualification, to start work and assisting instructors. We would need to log 60 dives before we could work, but we could do that during our travels, and once we got the qualification, it should allow us to fund our travels long term.

And so, for a while, some of the money we saved from lifeguarding went towards open water training in the grey, cold sea and water-filled quarries. British divers have a reputation amongst the best in the world, due to the conditions they are forced to train in. Wow, we thought: this would prepare us for anything.

Our first ever deep dive during our Advanced course was on a cold, dark winter's day at Dorothea Quarry in Llanllyfni. A large slate quarry in the wild Nantlle Valley, it was used from the 1820s until the 1970s, when it was flooded. Now you could be forgiven for thinking it was a natural lake, with steep grey cliffs at one end and enclosed by thick green trees, with forest stretching off into the hills. Yet on this cold, dark winter's day it had an eerie atmosphere, and even more so since I'd heard that its deep waters had taken the lives of scuba divers just two weeks before. In fact, over the decades, dozens had lost their lives. It was known for being very dark and cold, so much so that diving there unsupervised was frowned upon. But as a training venue with a qualified instructor, it was perfect.

We put on dry suits and tanks filled with compressed air – oxygen and nitrogen. The instructor gave us a timed maths test on a miniature whiteboard, which we strapped to our buoyancy control device so that we could repeat the test at the bottom. We braced ourselves for the chill, and dropped down to 30 metres. It didn't take long to understand what 'nitrogen narcosis' means. This is a drowsy, tipsy feeling induced by breathing certain gases under high pressure which, combined with the cold, affects the brain and slows the thinking, like an anaesthetic. We did the second maths test, aware that we were a lot slower this time. I looked around and above me: from far below the surface, everything seemed strangely amazing and I mumbled into my breathing regulator, "Holy shit!" They say scuba diving is the closest you can get to feeling as if you're in space. I was floating like an astronaut.

Advanced course: Tick.

Meanwhile, we were also busy getting visas and vaccinations, booking flights, managing our finances, making professional calls and emails – doing it all ourselves was developing us in small ways already. And suddenly it all happened. More than two years since the idea first came into my head, after 18 months of planning and saving, Mat and I had purchased all our gear and organised everything, and this was it. We held a farewell party, a big gathering of friends and family for food and drinks on a hot summer's day. I was going to miss my family but we'd stay in touch. It was time for Mat and me to make our way in the big wide world.

# 2: Adrenaline adventures in Asia and Australia

The alleyway was lit by hundreds of red lanterns, and lined with stalls plastered with placards advertising their wares in letters we couldn't begin to understand. Under the bright lights, vendors in red aprons shouted out to browsers both Chinese and foreign: "Hello! Hello! You want…?" We walked the packed aisles, pushing through the crowds to peer at stacks of skewered meat in every colour, trying to catch our first sight of such infamous street food as scorpion-on-a-stick.

Donghuamen Night Market in the Wangfujing district was well known as a weird food heaven.

"It's manic," the American guy in our hostel had said. So of course, we had to go.

It felt surreal to actually be in the big, busy city of Beijing, China: our first stop, the furthest I'd ever been away from home. You can imagine us, two lads from North Wales with crew cuts, Mat an inch taller with brown hair and eyes, me with dirty blonde hair and blue eyes, both totally buzzed up with big grins plastered on our faces, ready for adventure. As soon as we'd left the airport it had already felt like a different planet, with a huge crowd of people shouting out to offer lifts into the city – one guy even tapped on his bicycle seat offering us a "bunk" – and I loved it. It had been a dream for so long, and I already felt I'd achieved something huge just by getting here at the age of 19.

We'd taken the train, and stepping outside we were assailed by a wave of humid heat, sweat pricking our foreheads after only a couple of minutes. The city smelled of street food, sewage, flowers, cigarette smoke from guys playing cards in front of almost all kinds of shop, garbage, exhaust fumes and a random unidentifiable smell which seemed pretty much a fixture of the Beijing air. Bicycles shot out of alleyways to join busy roads, dodging the cars and cutting across them, horns blaring constantly not from road rage but habit.

Like walking the Great Wall, a visit to Donghuamen Night Market was seen as the thing you had to do as a tourist in Beijing. And just the smells of odd insects and animals frying were crazy enough. But I wasn't there just to look: I wanted to know what snake and scorpion and tarantula tasted like, because it went with my whole ethos of trying new things, exploring and pushing my boundaries. I was young and had a curious mind. So it was in at the deep end. We stopped at a stall bristling with things decidedly black and spidery-looking, I haggled with the vendor over the price and he handed me a tarantula to eat. It had a texture sort of like tuna. And having tried that, I went on to scorpion, which tasted like tiny, badly burned chicken nuggets. I tried snake, cricket, maggots… Some Americans stopped to watch, cringing and laughing, and some Chinese stopped and did the same, which surprised me. I probably wouldn't do it now because it feels a bit inappropriate and cruel, and in any case the market has closed down. But at the time it felt good to get that mad experience for just a few pounds, the price of a beer back home.

Trekking along part of the Great Wall of China was something I'd wanted to do for years. The scale of it appealed to me – the fact that it had been built by thousands of men to keep back the Mongolians during the Ming Dynasty, the history of two thousand years of construction, and the vastness of it. Whenever I thought of China, the Great Wall came to mind, and I wondered if one day I might walk the whole thing, something very few people had done. But for now we were just there to hike a few miles and I wanted to cover the untouched section, where we had to drop off the wall to get around the bushes that had grown over it. Whenever we ventured too far, the tour guide called us back.

We were on the tourist route, but at first it was great meeting so many different people. I often find that a good way to inject adventure into something is to go low-budget, and since we were keen to stretch out our travel funds anyway, we decided to travel from Beijing to Shanghai taking the cheapest transport available, which was the train. We bought the least expensive tickets possible, not realising at the time that we hadn't even paid for a seat. The train, quite old, had seen better days and we had to sit on the floor in the back, between a toilet leaking urine and a stinking bin used as a toilet for children and for the travel-sick to vomit in – for about 30 hours.

There was a constant stench from a toilet that was struggling to flush. We got zero sleep and I joked to Mat that we should jump off and buy bikes instead. But we weren't alone; there were locals who had to suffer this grim section with us, like fellow prisoners in a cell suffering our punishment together… We just had to brave it, and the people were really friendly, giving us bread and buns and hot dogs from ripped carrier bags. We couldn't understand each other but we exchanged smiles and hand gestures to make one another laugh throughout that long journey. At the end of the trip, we all shook hands and waved each other goodbye.

In Shanghai we met a Chinese guy called Chris at our hostel, and travelled around the city together, having a crazy night out before we headed further south to Hong Kong. This was way too expensive for us but we visited a huge shopping mall where TV screens outside the adventure shops played clips of surfing, wake boarding and other extreme sports. "I want some of that," I said to Mat, so we popped over to Macau to take on the world's highest bungee jump.

This wasn't a cheap adventure, but I'd never done a bungee jump before and this was a must-do activity for adrenaline nuts. There's something about extremes – the biggest and the best – that brings out my competitive spirit and if you can jump 233 metres off a building, you're challenging yourself to conquer your fears. We took the lift to the 61st floor. Mat and I flipped a coin; he lost, so had to go first – though as I watched him being strapped in and he pulled funny faces at me to mask his increasing nerves, I wondered whether going second was the right call after all. *Three, two, one…* He didn't hesitate and went for it, and I heard him screaming most of the way down.

My turn: they harnessed me in and looped my legs to the bungee cord. I held on to the railing and walked onto the ledge that stuck out from the top of the building, looking down at the cars and trucks that seemed so tiny below, a cold wind blowing around me. The rope dangled off the building, so heavy it was almost pulling me off. Mat hadn't hesitated so I had to match that. *Three, two, one... Bungee!* I threw myself off the building, shot down – it felt like eight or ten seconds to reach the bottom – before shooting back up again. I loved every second – what a buzz.

In Macau we had a pathetic attempt at gambling, since it's the second biggest casino city in the world, known as the Vegas of China. We'd never gambled in our lives and got just one chip, worth something like five pounds, which was a lot for us, but all the tables refused to let us play. It was too funny: this was a place for big spenders with music, dancers and bright lights. Having failed even to get our five pounds refunded we bought a beer each because we got a small bowl of peanuts with it, and we were happy with that. We made a toast to China: our two weeks there, mostly on the east coast, had been amazing and we hadn't even scratched the surface of this huge country. I knew I'd be back.

The next day we flew southeast to Thailand, starting off as most travellers do on the mad and marvellous Khao San Road in Bangkok with its food stalls, beer gardens, massage and tattoo parlours, night clubs, fortune tellers, gurus, con artists and more. Music blared and people shouted, trying to sell us odd things. It was familiar to me from watching *The Beach*, a film I'd loved, in which Leonardo DiCaprio travels through this country, hungry for unique experiences. That was what I was here for. After finding a place to stay that didn't have rats and cockroaches running about, we followed the sound of bass music beating in the distance. I felt the vibrations in my body as we grew closer. We reached the source of the sound to find a big festival, but I was curious about some high-pitched music I could hear a little further away.

I kept going and found a Muay Thai ring, with traditional music screeching away as two guys battled within. I'd heard of Muay Thai but never seen it. This was by far the most brutal combat I had ever witnessed, and I was in awe of the technique but also the sheer power of these guys who looked no bigger than myself. I thought that, one day, I would love to become a Muay Thai fighter.

We experienced the nightlife of Bangkok that night, all night through to the morning, then had to make a plan for what to do next. We ventured into a travel agency and asked the Thai agent about the best and cheapest dive spots. He was very helpful; he recommended Koh Tao, meaning "Turtle Island", where he said the diving was beautiful and inexpensive – a true paradise island where we could dive with the best school on the island, Bans Diving. We loved the sound of it and booked to leave the following day. Unfortunately we were victims of Bangkok's nightlife yet again that night and missed the bus, but we managed to leave later that evening, travelling to Chumphon by bus and then catching a boat, the whole journey taking about 12 hours. Koh Tao was indeed a stunningly beautiful island, just north of its bigger neighbours Koh Samui and Koh Pha-Ngan. It was a classic

Thai island, with lush forest covering the hilly interior, white sand trailing into clear, pale blue sea, plenty of budget accommodation and cool bars for chilling out.

While in North Wales we'd gone diving in trousers, jumpers and fleeces with a dry suit over the top; here it was just shorts or maybe a short-sleeved wet suit. I was in my element, dropping underwater for the first time in a while. The water was warm, rays of sun shining through the clear water to glint off objects at the bottom. Clear water meant high-definition visibility – we could see for over 20 metres. We'd relax on the boat in the sun, drink a fruit juice and drop down for a second dive, finish off with some fruit then later a good meal and drinks with dive buddies to talk about the day. I loved the atmosphere. Koh Tao was encircled by coral and the diving was varied, with an abundance of sites, and you could see sharks, clown fish, barracuda, stingrays and plenty more. It was the perfect place to log some dives.

One day a few of us were diving to about 18 metres on a hot, sunny day with deep blue skies. As you come up to break the surface, you're meant to drain the air out of your buoyancy control device (BCD), put one hand up above you and look up. I'd gone a good few months without diving, but doing it was jogging my memory about what I needed to do. As I was ascending, I looked at the other divers in the group, a short distance away from me, rather than where I was heading. I looked up at the last moment to see something above me – at first I wasn't sure what it was, but it didn't look right. Then it clicked: it was a huge jellyfish, about a foot in diameter, its tentacles dangling down a metre towards me – I was close to hitting them.

I just managed to kick away from it, avoiding what would have been a pretty grim ending to the dive. It was a close call. The others were too far away to see but I banged on my tank to get their attention and we all circled, in awe of this mighty, alien-looking thing. I often say I like to learn through experience, and try not to make the same mistake twice. After that, on every dive I always raised my hand and looked up when I was ascending – lesson learned.

Keen to continue with our travels, after logging a few dives we headed back to Bangkok. It was great making new friends from all over the world, and for a while we followed the other tourists pretty aimlessly, even visiting a zoo in Pattaya.

Then I was stricken with a mysterious illness. I was vomiting, had diarrhoea and red spots under the skin on my hand. It just got worse and although I couldn't eat, I continued to retch. I'd never felt like that before so I decided to go to a doctor, and the doctor thought it was dengue fever. He sent me straight back to the hospital in Bángkok, where I discovered I didn't have dengue fever after all – I had filariasis, also known as elephantiasis. It's contracted from mosquitoes that cause worms to lodge in the lymphatic system, where they gradually enlarge and obstruct the lymph flow, making particular areas of the body swell up massively, especially the legs and external genitals.

I'd caught it at an early stage and all it needed was a big injection in the bum and a few tablets, and the worms would come out of me when I went to the toilet. So that would be something to look forward to… As I walked out of the hospital I turned to see an old man with swollen limbs, obviously suffering what I had just been treated for – but due to lack of money, he had left the disease to progress to the point where it was untreatable. I wished I could help.

Thankfully I was back to normal quickly, but very wary now of those nasty little mosquitoes. Having crossed over the border to Siam Reap in Cambodia to visit Angkor Wat, we found ourselves in Phnom Penh on the banks of the Mekong River, sulking.

We were in a bad mood. With no-one to blame but ourselves, we'd trailed along the tourist conveyor belt for too long, getting ripped off a bit here and there. Being novice travellers, we'd made a miscalculation with currencies and spent far more than we anticipated. We also saw that however much fun we were having (when not dealing with worms in my blood), we were on the same trail as everyone else, from trekking with tourists on the Great Wall to visiting zoos to sit with tigers and partying a bit too much. We shared the same experiences, stories and photos as everyone else. It was supposed to be more wild and adventurous.

Contracting elephantiasis had perhaps been the wake-up call I needed to do something different. We had always spoken of doing mad adventures. We needed to find a cheap adventure that would be completely different and challenge us.

Suddenly, a thought popped into my head. It was something we had mentioned during the planning process, but had forgotten: the idea of cycling across a country. I mentioned it again to Mat – and suddenly we felt energised, as if this was what we'd been missing, that spirit of adventure, the nerves and excitement combined. We both snapped out of our moods. We were going to cycle Vietnam.

"But on what bikes?" said Mat.

And as he said this, we heard a screeching noise behind us in the distance, repeating itself. We turned around, and there was this skinny, frail old lady cycling up towards us on an incredibly rusty, cheap and bog-standard bike.

"Perfect," I said. "We'll get a couple of those."

And we laughed our heads off at the thought of seeing each other on one of those, and the humour put us back in a good mood, and we felt motivated all over again. All that remained was to find a couple of bikes.

We walked around the city on a hunt for the very cheapest, most basic bikes to be had: £10 each. They were new but ridiculous, with no gears or suspension. We laughed at the little bell and basket on the front and how delicately made they were; they were your typical old Vietnamese ladies' bikes to cycle to work every morning, most definitely not to cycle the entire length of a country. We couldn't stop laughing. I felt it fitting that we should name them; after all, we were going to spend a long time with them. So mine was called Elder and Mat named his Dot.

We cycled through the busy capital city of Phnom Penh to search for a tent, which we found for £5. Although not waterproof and possibly the worst tent a person could buy, it was good value for money and all we could afford. We also got a loaf of bread and some peanut butter. We found some string on the side of the road that we used to tie our rucksacks on to the racks. Then we spent no more than two minutes on Google, looking at the names of some of the villages and towns we would pass through *en route*, and we wrote them down in a list so that we'd be able to show the locals, and hopefully they could point us in the right direction. And that was it – we were ready.

We gave the bikes a trial run, cycling about 70km there and back to an orphanage where we helped out with odd jobs for a couple of days, fixing things or painting or playing football with the kids. By the time we'd cycled back, we reckoned the bikes might break down during the big cycle but they were good enough to start.

The locals in Phnom Penh, when they heard we planned to cycle over to Ho Chi Minh in the south of Vietnam and then up to the northern capital of Hanoi, said we couldn't do it. They said it was impossible for us to cross the border from Cambodia to Vietnam at that point, or to cycle that distance. It was ridiculous, they said. But we'd already decided. We said this is adventure; let's do it. They laughed at the bikes. We loved this and decided to go for it regardless. We knew there was a chance that we might be turned back at the border, but we'd figure it out when the time came. *Let's just focus on the now; let's start the journey.* And off we went.

With no map, no pump, no puncture repair kit, no helmets, lights or reflectors, we left late at night whilst it was cool. As we cycled out of the city, locals looked impressed to see us, and we got on well with everyone we met. Cycling is a popular mode of transport for them, and we were riding as the locals ride – no fancy gear, or Lycra, or bicycles kitted out with GPS – purely because we couldn't afford to do it any other way. We made the most of the wide open motorway, grabbing onto the back of slow-moving lorries after an enormous amount of effort and thoroughly enjoying the thrill of being pulled along. The police officers driving past didn't reprimand us but laughed at our foolishness.

We had done it, setting off only two days after the idea coming to mind. This is what adventure is all about, I told myself. We had over 1,130 miles of roads ahead of us; we didn't know what we would face or how tough it would be, yet we were on a huge buzz. I felt so alive. I was exploring this country which I was completely unfamiliar with alongside my best mate, far from the beaten track. The only tourists that we did see were the ones that would pass us in the middle of the night on their overland night coach whilst either sleeping or watching a movie. *That's no way to travel a country*, I thought; *look at all that they're missing!* As we cycled down a dirt road in Cambodia, the local kids ran out of the huts on either side, chasing us and shouting, "Hello!" Everyone was full of smiles and it felt truly special.

Had the people in the capital been right about the border? We arrived there late. Border control was closed. The guys re-opened it for us, which was very generous of them. And off we went.

We had so much energy that on some days after a long day's cycle, we'd continue through the night – the freedom of it was bliss. We ended up spray painting the bikes and even the pink bells, trying to make them look more manly, but failed miserably – they just looked more hilarious, and no amount of spray paint could disguise the twee baskets on the front.

We ate the same food as the locals, living off nothing but noodles and fizzy drinks, mainly Red Bull to keep us awake on our night-time rides. On occasion we'd treat ourselves to an egg or a sausage with our noodles, but if they seemed slightly overpriced, even by about 10 pence, we'd go without. Our budget was tight. One day we treated ourselves to an ice cream and set off cycling with them; when the ice cream fell off my cone onto the hot ground and started to melt, I was so unbelievably gutted, I had to cycle a kilometre back and get another.

Although we were carrying our £5 tent, we barely used it. On a couple of occasions we'd come across hammock shops, which were 20 pence for the night. Other nights we'd find a super-cheap hotel that stayed open late for the lorry drivers.

And of course we only had shorts and vests to wear the whole way, even when we were at Da Lat in the highlands of Vietnam, where it was pretty cold and everyone else was wearing woolly hats and jackets, looking at us and wrapping their arms around their bodies as if to say, "It's cold up here!" Then we were cycling down to Nha Trang on the coast and it was dark – it went dark quite early, about five or six o'clock – and a thunderstorm hit, and it was absolutely throwing it down, though it was still quite warm. Soaked through, we stood up on the pedals, howling into the darkness, "Whooooh! YEEEEEE-HAAAAA!"

I said to Mat as we were cycling, "It would be awesome to have a world map at the end of my days, marked up with not only countries I'd visited but the expeditions and adventures that I'd taken on." I envisaged a mix of hard-core, non-motorised survival expeditions across the globe, crossing jungles, traversing deserts, cycling countries and kayaking rivers.

It was just a brief chat but one that stuck with me. In several ways Vietnam was the catalyst for a lot of the adventures to come, because it made me feel truly alive. When you exercise and train, it sets off endorphins that make you feel positive. There we were, in the rain, it was dark, we were soaked through and we had bin bags over our feet… But because I was cycling, exercising, I felt alive and started thinking about things I could do in the future.

Cycling was great, but as long as you have a road in front of you, it will take you through villages and cities, places where food, water and help are almost always available. In Vietnam, there was always someone around to help, and they were resourceful and hard-working – I noticed almost every hut had a shed extension where the man of the house kept his tools. Whenever we developed punctures in the dead of night, we'd get off and push until we reached a hut where the family was awake.

Once we came across a small hut where the whole family was still up at 2am, and when the Vietnamese guy saw my bike tyre, with most of the tools already in his pocket, he simply fixed it with ease and waved us goodbye. I've always had great faith in humankind. It doesn't always go to plan, of course, but if you're respectful and polite, then you'll usually get back what you give.

When we'd stop for lunch in small villages, the word would spread and before we knew it, the whole village would be gathered around us. The locals would approach us whilst we were eating and laugh at our sun-bleached leg and arm hair. I realised that I'd not seen any men with leg hair, so they were fascinated. As we tried to eat, they'd start yanking hairs out of our legs – it got quite painful!

It became quite dangerous at times on the road. We were hit by mopeds and chased by dogs. The flies sent us crazy, continually buzzing around every orifice, and we were battered by strong headwinds. It was often hot during the day, sometimes over 40°C, but night threw thunderstorms our way. But we pushed on through all of this, the bikes breaking down 17 times in total. Huge lorries honked their horns from behind us at 3am, scaring the hell out of us every time and causing us to sway in all directions and go from sleepy to panicked in a second.

One night I actually fell asleep whilst cycling. Mat was falling asleep too and it was only the collision of our two bikes that stopped me from veering into the middle of the road, seconds before a lorry went speeding past, blaring its horn – another close call.

It took us about 15 days to cycle from Cambodia up to north Vietnam. As we finally neared the end, we were starting to miss easy access to different foods so the last stint to Hanoi saw us cycle 39 hours straight – we were both so excited about getting there. It was tough to stay awake, and dangerous. We finally saw the city in the distance, about 12km away, which would normally only take an hour or two; but it seemed to take forever, it was such a hot day. We'd race to each bridge and rest in the shade before pushing on, our forearms melting and our skin badly sun-burned.

When we finally made it three hours later, we were turned down by seven hostels and guest houses. Fortunately, as we were losing all hope of finding a comfy bed, a kind lady took pity on us and allowed us to stay at her guest house.

It was only then that we saw ourselves in a mirror and realised why we'd been turned away: we had flies stuck in our hair, some of them still living; bloodshot eyes from the dust, blue skin from the mosquito spray of the night mixed with the sun screen of the day;

and bags under our eyes from going more than 45 hours without any sleep – we looked half-dead. We hit the deck after getting a good wash and eating all we could.

For the next few days we couldn't stop talking about our cycle trip. Doing it with such a low budget had given it an extreme edge. I had filmed it on a very cheap and nasty camera, and we looked through the footage in disbelief that we had just cycled Cambodia and Vietnam on those bikes, proving wrong those people who had told us it was impossible. We placed the bikes against a railing in Hanoi, hoping someone would make good use of them. As we travelled on to Laos, on a bus this time, I continued to think about it. It was the best thing I had ever done. I realised that I had found my passion, my niche; I was shocked to see how much I'd overcome and now had a hunger to keep pushing myself. I couldn't stop.

So I didn't.

That quite dangerous adventure was the catalyst, the one that got me hooked.

I'd been fascinated for a long time by the idea of experiencing different cultures – different ways of life, far from how we live in the Western world. Partly influenced by stories I'd been told or documentaries I watched, I wanted to learn from tribal communities who still hunt and gather and work solidly as a team, sharing knowledge in order to survive in a harsh and remote environment; to learn by being with them and taking part. And so when an opportunity came up, in northern Thailand, to go into the jungle and learn some survival skills, we agreed right away and set off the next day.

On the first day we trekked through the jungle, covering a good distance, hunting and gathering from the land, washing and drinking from rivers and waterfalls. It was humid and the loud, high-pitched noises of insects surrounded us. The local Thai guide warned us to watch out for any venomous snakes that might be lurking. We constructed our own shelter at night, hacking down bamboo with a machete to make the base, then using the outer shards of the bamboo to tie it together and create a roof. We collected banana leaves, just one from each plant rather than take too many from a single one, and tied them into the roof at an angle to keep us dry if it rained.

We also used banana leaves for sleeping mats and built a fire close by to keep us warm, cook our food, and make smoke to keep flies and mosquitoes away. We fished in the nearby river using just stripped bamboo as a rod, with a small hook attached to the end; there was nothing you couldn't do with bamboo, said our guide, who loved it so much that he named his son Bamboo. We also gathered mushrooms and banana flowers, which are edible along with the stem, and added all this to the fish we caught to make a nutrient-packed soup.

We slept soundly, and next morning I awoke to an army of red ants marching down the ridge of my banana leaf bed, six inches from my face. I raised my head and looked around, couldn't see any ants on my body, and went back to sleep. With no bites, I let them be, and enjoyed the feeling of being at one with nature.

We walked a solid nine hours that day, collecting melon and corn to eat for energy as we continued to hack our way through the bush. Our guide told us we were "strong characters for the jungle". We saw how knowledgeable he was, and how well adapted to his environment. Learning just a fraction of his skills was an honour.

We eventually crossed over into Myanmar and made it to an isolated Burmese hill tribe, living on top of rolling hills surrounded by jungle. Nobody could speak English within the community; some kept their distance whilst others smiled and waved at us. We went off to collect berries that act as a mosquito repellent once burst and rubbed into your skin, and learned how to set up a snare for squirrel, catching one and bringing it back to base, skinning it and placing it whole into our melon soup. It tasted great, a chewy version of frog or chicken, and was just what we needed after a big day.

Soon after, Mat and I laughed at each other when we discovered the toilet was a tiny dark hut where you let loose within a small bucket, with another bucket full of dirty water beside it to wash your backside. It was horrendous – I needed to go and couldn't hold on, whilst Mat was outside laughing at me. I shrugged my shoulders and thought, oh well – I better get used to it.

I realised there was a side of me that wanted to do more of this. I'd begun breaking more into my "wild side". I wasn't too bothered about the rats, cockroaches, spiders and other creepy crawlies, just as I wasn't particularly missing nice foods or creature comforts and luxuries. I felt I'd toughened up a little over the past couple of months, had faced everything and risen to the challenge. It was still early days but I could sense myself feeling more at home in changing environments and circumstances.

***

As we left Asia for Australia, we knew we'd have to start working to earn some cash to fund the travels. In Darwin in the Northern Territory, our first job was the standard seasonal work of fruit picking. It's pretty easy to find fruit-picking jobs. Why? Because no-one lasts long at it.

It was physically demanding in horribly hot weather and the bosses were tough; the guy shouted at you if you dropped a mango. They tried to motivate us to work 18 hours by saying at the end they'd treat all of us workers to a barbecue, so we all kept going at the thought of a decent feast. Then, when it came to it, we got one hot dog each. Devastating! We were sick of it pretty quickly.

Mat flew to Melbourne in the south, where he had a job offer, and I wanted to head east. While fruit-picking I had met two great guys, Dan Gardener from Australia and Manuel Huber from Germany, and the three of us decided to take in an adventure by driving the worst roads possible around 1,900 miles from Darwin to Cairns. Dan had said how extreme the Northern Territory was and so, prepared for the worst case scenario and the chance of a breakdown in the middle of nowhere, we packed the car with extra gasoline, water and food – as well as a few-months-old puppy that Dan was looking after.

We were on a dirt track that was only open for six months of the year, and because winter and the rainy season were approaching, most of the cars had taken the winter route, which is a longer way round but a lot safer. We were in a rusted-out old car that wasn't too good for the conditions we took it through – extremely muddy, crossing rivers, the roads getting worse and worse. Any road we couldn't see on the map, we'd always take, in the hope it would provide us with a more adventurous route, and it certainly did. A couple of times the car sank in the mud; sometimes we had to wait a couple of hours for a 4x4 to come by and pull us out. We did well and got pretty far, but eventually we broke down for good in the middle of the outback.

The three of us turned to each other with looks of shock, then started laughing. We now had to think carefully. We were warned by the previous guy in a 4x4 that he hadn't seen another car pass this route in a good week or so. We pushed the car off the track into the bush, gathered our belongings and the extra water we brought with us, and placed a piece of card next to a full tank of gasoline saying: "Use me, We've broken down and walked on. Please pick us up."

Excited about what would happen next, we left the car behind and walked up ahead in search of water. When it got too hot, Dan and Manuel stayed on the side of the road in the shade and I pushed on a little more. It started to get dark quite fast and just as I was about to turn back, I saw a family of kangaroos. They froze, looking directly at me, and I did exactly the same: we caught each other's eye and it was amazing. Then they loped off in the other direction.

Just as I got back to Dan and Manuel, a massive thunderstorm hit from out of nowhere, which brought us exactly what we were looking for – water! We pinned up a shelter at an angle where we could fill up four bowls of water at once. Then I pulled out my legendary non-waterproof two-man tent from Cambodia and we all squeezed inside it, soaked through but warm, and eventually dropped off to sleep.

Thirteen hours later, the first car approached. The guy was cautious when he saw us all on the track waving him down, but he gradually slowed down and wound down his window just an inch or two at most. There was a big pit bull in the back of his truck. When we told him what had happened, he said, "Blimey, jump in.

"I'm not leaving you out here," he said. "There's an aboriginal tribe just across the way and they don't much like white people. You're lucky they didn't find you."

We realised that however prepared we thought we were, it could have been a stupid and irresponsible adventure after all. But for the next six days, we continued hitchhiking and camping. Dan said we needed to split up as people tended not to pick up three male hitchhikers together. So Dan went alone, taking the puppy, while Manuel and I stuck together. We were picked up by some nice people and some slightly crazy, drunken and creepy, people who looked like serial-killers, but we made it to Cairns.

We did more fruit picking there in Togrog, living in a tent to save money. They didn't like us much because we weren't paying for their accommodation; they thought we were cheapskates, and we had a few arguments. After Asia, it hit me that Australia was a really expensive place. Mat said there was plenty of work in Melbourne so I decided to meet him down there. Eventually I got an interview for a sales job, selling contracts door-to-door for Australian Power and Gas. Two hundred people were interviewed for six jobs over the course of a week, so I have no idea how I got picked, but I winged it and got the job.

And so I found myself in the strange position of going door to door in temperatures over 30°C wearing black trousers, black shoes and a shirt, with an overweight and unhealthy boss called Jeremy who was there to make sure I did my job properly. On the first morning, we were driving to our area for the day with some other guys. Suddenly Jeremy went berserk, screaming at the guy who was driving that he'd missed the turning. It turned out we'd missed the turnoff for KFC and had to turn back to load up on greasy fast food for breakfast. I couldn't have been further from my Burmese Hill Tribe experience if I'd tried.

On one particular day, we got to a house and Jeremy said, "OK, watch me, watch how I sell."

We started walking up a long drive, and at the end was a guy doing pull-ups on a bar attached to the wall, his muscles rippling. Jeremy started his selling pitch, and the guy stood by, listened quietly and politely for a while then put his hand up, saying, "Look, I appreciate it, but I'm already locked into a contract. Thanks anyway, though. I appreciate what you guys do. It's not easy, walking around in this temperature, and I know you rely on commission so you need to get people to sign up."

Jeremy came back at him with some flippant and fairly disrespectful comment about how much commission he made, rubbing his fingers together in the universal symbol of money as he mentioned the type of upmarket car he drove. I just cringed.

The guy replied, "It's not all about the money, though, is it? You need the lifestyle too. You need the balance."

It hit me. He was completely right. I'd been all about that my whole life. What was I doing standing suited up with a guy like Jeremy, sucked into the business path, which was motivated only by money?

It shook me up, woke me up. So when, a day or two later, Jeremy announced that he wanted to take me to Brisbane to work with him, I realised I didn't want to go. I told Mat, who had a job cleaning swimming pools, that I was quitting.

"I might as well be back home lifeguarding as doing this," I said. "You don't like your job. I don't like mine. We're on a low budget. How about we do it again?"

"Do what again?"

"Let's buy the cheapest bikes we can find…"

All at once the adventure spirit came flooding back in and we were hooked. We made a deal, quit our jobs, and two weeks later, all buzzed up and excited, Mat and I set off again: from Melbourne to Adelaide, covering some 700 miles over 12 days, allowing us to see more of the country whilst soaking up the Australian wilderness.

I had to buy another bike – a women's mountain bike, as it was the cheapest. I bought a pink helmet for a laugh, having been dared to by Manuel, who had come down to Melbourne a few days earlier. It went well with the pink and white bike. After buying a rack and a front basket, it cost around £70. Again we took minimal provisions and the same tent I had used in Vietnam was my home each night, as accommodation was so expensive in Australia. It usually ended up wet inside as it wasn't waterproof, especially after a cat attacked it one night, piercing big holes in it.

The route took us along the Great Ocean Road allowing

to see the "Twelve Apostles" – a dramatic, seemingly endless coastline with sheer cliffs and limestone stacks rising up out of the ocean. Heading further inland, we saw wildlife in abundance in its natural habitat: porcupines, snakes, kangaroos, wallabies, koalas, emus, dingo, parrots... One morning, I found a poisonous whiteback spider crawling on my hand, and had to flick it off. But the only thing that bothered us was the flies, which were so energy-draining; we'd do anything to get away from the pesky things.

The distances were immense and at one point we were severely dehydrated and desperate for water after cycling seven hours in 44°C with only 100ml of water to share between us, so when we came across a sealed water tank, we licked the condensation drops off the outside. Completely exhausted and breathing heavily, we looked at each other in disbelief at just how hot and tired we were, when a fly landed on Mat's tooth, which instantly had us in stitches again.

Like the Vietnam cycle, trip the Australian one was a last-minute decision and tough mainly due to the unsuitable bikes and lack of equipment, but both journeys were massive highlights of my travels. In Australia the winds were against us almost every day. But what I was learning was that if you challenge yourself physically and mentally, you start to understand just how much you can push your body and mind. We had thought of continuing to Perth, crossing the country, but Mat had heat exhaustion and his bike broke, so he had to hitchhike on the last day to Adelaide, and we decided we couldn't go on.

We still had nine months left on our once-in-a-lifetime

12-month Australian work visa, but we'd started missing Asia – the food, how cheap it was, everything about it. I loved the people who were so laidback, fun and understanding, who always had time for you – I would always have time for them. Australia had quite strict rules, like a warmer version of the UK: Mat had been fined after being caught cycling with his helmet hanging off his handlebars. We missed the craziness and the lack of "Health and Safety".

So we decided to go to India.

# 3: Becoming a dive master and Muay Thai fighter

It was a 24-hour drive from New Delhi to Srinagar in Kashmir, close to northern India's border with Pakistan, and I've still never met a crazier driver than that guy. He drove the 24 hours without a break. He was clearly very tired, but he wouldn't stop driving. We were on a narrow road, with the steep side of a mountain on one side and a sheer drop on the other. It was too narrow to turn back. Lorries sped along and as our driver seemed to fall asleep at the wheel, we veered across the road almost hitting them. I held tight.

"You need to pull over and sleep," I said, thinking we could use one of the passing places to rest.

He shook his head. "It's only four more hours." It seemed quite a lot when you've already been driving for 20. Eventually I managed to make him pull over and sleep for a few hours before continuing, and we made it without a major mishap.

Srinagar is a magnificent ancient city high in the mountains, cool and peaceful, and we stayed on the lake in a houseboat run by a guy called Ali. The call to prayer rang out at sunset and we were surrounded by snow-capped Himalayan peaks – on a misty evening, it made us yearn to trek up a mountain. But Ali said we needed a permit. I shrugged this off, saying we only wanted to walk up to the peaks nearby and couldn't afford a permit, but he replied that the Pakistan army controlled the border over there, and they wouldn't hesitate to shoot if we were trekking without permission. But we said to ourselves no, that's silly, we'll be completely fine.

"Well," he concluded, "I am telling the truth. If they see you, you must pray for your life. You must get on your knees, put your thumbs behind your ears." He told us a phrase meaning 'have mercy on me', which we should repeat. "And don't look into their eyes, look to the ground."

It was worrying, but the mountains were too tantalisingly close to give up the idea. We set out with a girl called Tess, who had also been staying at Ali's. As we walked through the town, the locals stopped to look at us, which put us on edge. Did they know?

It was just a day's hike through the valleys, where we saw huge glaciers and birds of prey circled above us; we believed there were rare snow leopards deeper in the mountain range. As we began working our way up higher, Tess turned back – maybe it was altitude sickness, or maybe she was nervous after everything Ali had said. A while later, we started to hear the sound of a helicopter. Mat and I looked at one another. Was it the Pakistan army, looking for us? I was wearing a bright red shirt, so I tore it off in panic and jumped into a bush to hide.

But after the helicopter disappeared, we continued and made

it to one of the peaks, and it just gave us an appetite for more. So after returning to Srinagar, we decided to go further into the Himalayas and two days later we took another car journey for four or five hours on high, narrow roads right up north to near the border with Pakistan, where we stayed with a local family. When I explained to the hut-owner, who was also a guide, that we wanted to trek to a peak, he said it was dangerous now, at the end of the winter. No-one had summited the peak we were looking at in this season.

On a bright morning, as we left, the sun reflected off the snow and filled the valley with golden light, the hills a patchwork of brown, green and yellow against the deep blue sky. Compared to the city of Delhi a few days earlier, it was now fresh, cool and open, the smell of pine flooding our nostrils, and it was so still and quiet that we could hear locals working in their huts further down the mountain, and the sound of rivers flowing through the valleys. Birds chirped in the forest and we saw a wild mountain chicken fly overhead. The guide led us up to about 4 – 5,000 metres above sea level, all steep climbing, zig-zagging our way up and around other mountains towards the peak. When we got to about two hours away from the summit, he stopped. He said he would go no further, and recommended we turn back also. We probably should have listened, but we could see the top and knew it wasn't far. He stayed to wait for us, and we carried on.

It was awkward and tiring to walk through the deep snow; any path there might have been was now buried, and we were ill prepared in terms of clothing, wearing just fleeces for warmth and some pretty ruined shoes. But we knew it would take us only a couple more hours to reach the top, so pushed on as fast we could in order to stay warm, and to get over this area where the snow-pack seemed unstable, on a slope steep enough for an avalanche to be triggered. We crossed that section and pushed up towards the peak, resting every ten steps or so. The snow was up to our knees, sometimes deeper, so it was a slow process, but we reached the summit, and it was something special to be level with the mountains surrounding us. It was so peaceful, Mat and I had to high-five each other and shout, "WHOOOOO!" as we took in the 360-degree view from the top. We soon realised heavy clouds were coming in fast, foggy and misty, and we prepared to leave. Being stuck in a whiteout and not being able to find your way back is very dangerous. Then we began to hear loud thunder and roaring.

"That's not thunder," I said to Mat, "that's avalanches on other mountains."

We hurried back down. It was one of those close calls, of which there were many, and afterwards we thought, *We were lucky, but we probably shouldn't have done that*. But we found our guide waiting for us and we worked our way down, cold and hungry but filled with a sense of achievement. However reckless, however dangerous it had been, it was the best walk I had ever done. And that feeling would influence my future choices.

After that, it was time to immerse ourselves in local culture again. And in Varanasi, that was mad. The streets were filled with more pungent aromas than anywhere I had experienced before: the smells of spices, herbs, and chilli powder so intense you could almost taste it in the air. We loved the cheap food stands, and stopped to feast continually for 50 pence a meal. Cows were respected and left alone, even if they had wandered into the middle of a shop. One day we were strolling down one of the many winding, narrow alleyways overhung with washing, with just enough room to walk side by side, when suddenly we heard shouting and screaming and turned around to see a bull two metres behind us, trapped and panicked and heading straight towards us. We pressed ourselves to the wall and felt the heat of the animal as it pushed past. But there was more.

In the holy city, colourful buildings of all shapes and sizes crowd the banks of the Ganges, and steps known as ghats lead down to the water's edge, with drying laundry and pipes leading from men's urinals. There are cremation sites and, as the bodies burn, a head might drop off or a limb fall into the murky grey-brown water and bob off down the river to where a mother will be washing clothes and lads leaping into the river for a laugh. It's the most polluted river in the world, a dumping ground for everything from sewage to factory waste, but bathing in it is a sacred rite for the Hindus, to wash away their sins – a rite dating back to when the water was clean enough to drink – and I wanted to try going in just as the locals did.

There's a special technique: wade in, cover your nostrils and ears, close your mouth and eyes, and duck down quickly. Mat and I walked in, clearing a path through floating objects, and I went to move what looked like a thick rope out of my way. As I picked it up I realised it was faeces and threw it off, disgusted. Mat just laughed at me. We still went in, though it stank, and everything about it felt wrong: the water was warm like dirty bathwater and as I stepped in, my feet sank into goodness-knows-what, a thick mud-like gunge. I got on with it, dunked my whole body and came back up laughing at how grim it was, bits of material stuck to my body as I clambered out and made a beeline for the shower.

We'd wanted the craziness of Asia – and that's what we had got. But we were on the backpacker trail again, and even as we ventured further south to Goa, thinking about going to Sri Lanka and then on to Africa or South America, the money was running out and it was time to think long-term. I suggested we go back home while we still had a few thousand, go back to working as lifeguards to build up our money again, and then have more options about where to go and what to do next. So in 2011, after 10 months of travelling, we went home to North Wales and got our jobs back.

After the riot of colour and hot sun of India, it took some adjusting to be back – to go from the beautiful madness of the Ganges to a chlorinated and controlled swimming pool. I kept reminding myself it was only temporary, but after the initial excitement of seeing friends and family and eating foods I'd missed, I started to feel low. It hit me that what I missed was not just the travel, but the adventures. So I decided to discover England in the same way as I'd explored other countries. I set myself a challenge to cycle from John O'Groats to Land's End, solo and unsupported, close to a thousand miles in under 10 days. And to give it a purpose I chose to raise funds for a charity, the NSPCC. I set off with a cheap tour/race bike, minimal provisions, a small tent and a map which was completely useless.

It was a fantastic trip, camping along the way, averaging 130 miles a day. On three occasions I ended up in a city where they wouldn't allow camping, so I knocked on doors asking local residents if I could pitch my tent in their gardens. Only once did I get looked at like I was a complete freak – most people were very friendly. The scenery varied from mountain ranges to beautiful coastlines. On the last day, I covered a distance of 204 miles. I finished the journey from the north to the south of Britain, covering a distance of 985 miles, in seven days. And while I was cycling, I thought about what I was going to do next.

When I came back home, Mat and I sat in the conservatory of my house with a cup of tea. I said, "I've got a really exciting idea. And I think you might want to come along."

He picked up on my excitement and the sparkle in my eye. "What? What are you thinking?!"

"Remember when we were on Koh Tao in Thailand?" I said. When we were diving, I'd met a guy training for his Dive Master qualification. He'd said Koh Tao was a great place in the world to do it: a cheap and fun place to live, with great deep diving. "I'm going to live in Koh Tao and become a Dive Master."

If we completed our courses up to instructor level, I said, we could work and live abroad. And straight away, Mat loved it. So after five months of working hard to save some money, Mat having saved enough in the meantime to go to Canada to train as a skiing instructor, we both met out in Thailand. We went straight to Koh Tao, excited about the new chapter.

\*\*\*

Having come straight from a job in the UK, I was hungry for adventure. But I needed to focus on getting my qualification; I needed to work. For two months I followed the course at Davy Jones' Locker and logged 60 dives, then was offered a job as a Dive Master. I was soon teaching people to dive in some of the most exquisite waters in Asia, living on a beautiful, small island in the Gulf of Thailand and Andaman Sea, and meeting people from around the world, all receptive to new experiences and fun. The ocean was my office, and I wore nothing but shorts.

My favourite location was Chumphon Pinnacle, a 40-minute boat ride from the island, well known as one of the best spots around. The pinnacle dropped to over 40 metres deep and was home to an abundance of big aquatic life: you'd often see whale sharks and bull sharks and for me, that was what it was all about. The buzz when we got back in the boat would be huge: everyone had shared a fantastic experience and we'd all connect and form a bond. There was partying after, which I also loved – it was a good crowd and nightlife was dirt cheap. The lifestyle was amazing – sun, sea and extreme sport – and during time off we'd go on treks or rent a quad bike, and I learned how to do back flips. I met a few girls whom I connected with, just briefly because they were travelling and had to go home. A dream job by all accounts: what more could a man wish for?

The next step was to qualify as an instructor. I passed the course, then continued to become a master scuba diving trainer and specialty trainer so I could teach people how to dive in wrecks, how to deep dive, how to dive at night and how to dive with underwater scooters. They all offered different experiences and required different techniques, but there was something special about night diving. When it's pitch black and you can only see where your torch shines as you drop to the depths, it's easy to become disorientated, and important to stay focused. As you develop, you know what to look for. The ocean is even more alive at night, as that's when most aquatic life is out on the hunt. On one night dive, as I turned to look behind me, I saw I was being followed by a giant barracuda, a large predatory fish with a long, slender body and a large jaw and teeth. It was pretty eerie.

As a scuba diving instructor, I developed a strong sense of self and my confidence soared thanks to the connections and responsibilities. When I was invited to a tiny island down south called Koh Lipe with better diving, I said yes right away, leaving the nightlife of Koh Tao behind for a while. It would take only ten minutes to jog across Koh Lipe and it didn't have a fully functional ATM or 7–11 or even a proper boat pier, but it was a beautiful, pure island, a tranquil place. One day, heading out for a dive, we came across two huge whales, maybe Minke whales. I left my dive kit on the boat, and dived straight into the water with just a snorkel, fins and mask, and we spent the day swimming with eight-metre whales.

I lived there for three months, earning more money, concentrating on my fitness, eating healthy food – fruit, muesli and yoghurt for breakfast, rice and chicken for dinner – diving in the sun and training hard in the evening, which kept me focused and alert. I had a structured routine and I was feeling stronger than ever.

On Koh Tao, I'd started training as a Muay Thai fighter. That fight I'd seen in Bangkok had stuck with me. I've always believed that it's important to know how to defend yourself; I'm fascinated with fully understanding my body's capabilities and being able to use it to the best of its potential. Boxing, which I'd done in college, had been an excellent foundation for this, but I wanted to up my game and learn how to use more of the whole body. Muay Thai, an intense and brutal combat, is known as the martial art of eight limbs and would teach me stand-up grappling and strikes using the knees, legs, elbows and fists.

I trained in over 30°C, and competed against the locals in club fights. I loved the competition and the buzz of it. I learned how to beat my shins against wood to kill off nerve endings, and even when I wasn't training, at night I'd use the ridge of a book to hit my shins. Muay Thai is said to be the world's most devastating martial art, and I loved it. And when the season ended on Koh Lipe and I returned to Koh Tao, I had my first stadium fight.

It was in an outdoor venue with a shelter above, old-school, and all the Davy Jones' Locker guys had come out to support me. One of the fighters came from the mainland and was undefeated. I wasn't supposed to be fighting him, but the guy I was slated to fight didn't turn up and since we were the two headline fighters, it was on. I was nervous, but had been training hard five or six days a week. I was called up and jumped over the ropes, into the ring. The traditional Muay Thai music played, which I'd grown to appreciate, although it's intimidating. Played with high-pitched instruments and drums, it increases in tempo to encourage the combatants to fight.

I circled the ring, showing my respect. The other guy was acting in a pretty cocky way, confident the fight was his. It got me more fired up and fuelled. Locals were gathered around the ringside, with money in their raised hands, shouting – most pointing at my opponent, betting on him to win the fight, though a few were pointing my way, putting money on me to win. The shouting, cheering and music all started to fade as we walked into the centre. The referee went through the rules, grabbed our gloves and made us touch, then we walked back to our own corners. The bell went.

Most Thais think that Westerners are only good at punching and not kicking, so I'd been concentrating on perfecting my kicks. I came in with a head kick which he just managed to block but it still hit him. We circled each other before I went in for another head kick, catching him. He went for a low kick which I blocked but he left himself completely open, so I went in with a left straight punch, and it sent him down. He didn't get up after ten seconds, and it was classed as a technical knockout – not so surprising when you think that with the lack of Health and Safety, the gloves I was wearing were so old that the padding was all bunched on either side so it was pretty much like hitting with bare knuckles. I'd won my first stadium fight with a 12-second technical knockout in the first round. With everyone there in the crowd supporting me, and with my winning the equivalent of £100, life felt good.

I had spent a year and a half in paradise. But I was feeling too comfortable, too much in a routine. I was never going to settle in Thailand long term as a diver; it was a qualification that I now always had, something to fall back on if all else failed – but it was a stepping stone to the next big thing. Eventually I could ignore the adventure bug no longer. I had a calling, a desire to do something different. I wanted to undertake a bigger expedition than I'd ever done before. Mat and I had always got on well and we'd gone through all our years of travelling with not one argument; while scuba diving in caves or wrecks, we'd looked after each other. But maybe it was time to do something alone.

An idea had come to me of doing a trip in Mongolia. When I was young I had watched clips of the country: eagles hunting down rodents, foxes and even wolves; I was entranced by the scenery, the harsh landscape. I used to talk to my uncle Luke and we would say, "Imagine walking in the middle of Mongolia, against all the extreme conditions, fighting off wolves to stay alive." It had stayed with me. Although I met travellers constantly while living in Thailand, I hadn't met anyone who had been to Mongolia; no-one had even mentioned it, and I knew nothing about the country. That was part of its appeal. It was off the tourist track, which got me excited and curious. I couldn't stop thinking about it. It consumed me. It was like an itch I couldn't reach, an uncontrollable urge that needed fulfilling.

The only other thing I knew about Mongolia was that it had extreme weather and unforgiving terrain, which could provide me with the ultimate challenge. I'd done a few cycle trips and I liked the idea of a walk in an isolated place, survival-based, relying on myself. I remembered the exhilaration I'd felt on reaching those peaks in the Himalayas, and before that, the sense of peace I'd felt while living among the Burmese hill tribe. A walk seemed old school and meant I didn't have to stick to any roads. At first I considered a 100-mile trek; then I thought, why not trek from north to south? Gradually the distance of the walk crept upwards and it wasn't too long before the thought came to my head of walking the entire length of the country.

Mongolia became my project, my passion. I had found a country with barely any roads, a country that was extreme in every way from weather to terrain, and one I knew barely anything about.

The next few months were spent doing extensive research. If there was no work available, I'd see that as an opportunity to crack on with plans. Diving became a chore as all I wanted was to be moving things forward with the expedition. If the guys invited me out partying, I was no longer that interested – I was focused, and saw the Muay Thai fighting as a way to prepare myself.

I found out that Mongolia was the third most sparsely populated country in the world. Walking from west to east across mountains and desert would be something extraordinary.

I had planned carefully for this moment; all my previous adventures fed my hunger and inspiration. I really, really wanted this. That was my driving force.

# Part Two:
# WALKING ACROSS
# MONGOLIA

## My route across Mongolia

# 4: Being told it was impossible and going ahead anyway

My goal, then, was to do a solo and unsupported walk across the length of Mongolia, trekking through the Altai Mountains, on through the Gobi Desert and then into the steppe. When I started to plan, I thought it would be best to find someone who'd done it and ask for advice and tips, pick their brains about any dangers to be prepared for. I was struggling to find someone and it popped into my head that maybe I would be the first.

I wasn't in it for the record, but I couldn't find any evidence to suggest that anyone had completed a solo and unsupported walk across Mongolia. However, I found Ripley Davenport, who had attempted it and got just over halfway before he was evacuated due to an injury, abandoning the expedition at the 1,012-mile mark. I was in awe of his achievement but at the same time worried; Ripley had been in the Navy, was a desert explorer and had much greater experience than I had. I hadn't even been to a desert before, let alone walked across one. I started to doubt myself, as I read up on many of his struggles and heard he was stalked by grey wolves for two weeks. I reached out to him by email, asking for advice, and luckily he was nice enough to respond. It was a very intimidating response:

"You need to watch out for the dry wells, the stagnant water, the drunken nomadic drifters, the grey wolves, the snowstorms, the sand blizzards…"

It was enough to freak me out and get me to start looking at the world map again, maybe changing my mind and trying something different, in a more populated and safer country… I now saw this as a much bigger challenge than anticipated, but I was determined not to be put off. Ripley also wrote:

"Incredible is the ability to continue no matter what."

Those seemed like wise words, and I would remember them.

I thought the next step would be to contact someone in the country. Through my uncle I found a guy called Rob Mills who was at that point the manager of The Adventurists, a well-known company running adventures in and out of Mongolia. I contacted Rob and asked if he thought it was possible to walk the length of Mongolia solo and unsupported. At first he didn't think so, but was more than happy to help with the logistics of the expedition.

I was still in Thailand and there was a massive amount to organise. I'd submitted a proposal to apply for a £5,000 National Geographic grant, but that wasn't guaranteed; I'd passed the first stage and had been shortlisted, but wouldn't find out if I succeeded or not until early 2014. I had a few Skype meetings with Rob and after doing research with his team, and my dad and I contacting Guinness World Records and doing research of our own, there was no evidence to suggest that anyone had completed the walk across the country alone and unsupported.

Rob said that if I completed this expedition, I would be the first recorded person ever to do so. This changed everything for me; I took it far more seriously now and wanted it more than anything in the world. Not only would it be one heck of a challenge and experience, but there would be one huge reward at the end – being the first person in the world to achieve it. I started looking at it as more than just an adventure, possibly a career-changer. Taking on big expeditions had been my dream "job" since a youngster, but I'd never believed there would be a way to make it happen; it's not the kind of thing careers advisors suggest in school.

I needed to give up my life in Thailand, sell everything, and take a big risk by moving back to the UK to plan my Mongolia adventure. It was a make or break decision because if I failed to complete my Mongolian mission, I'd have to buy all the dive kit again. But I wouldn't fail. I couldn't let that happen. So I had to be 100 percent ready.

I had planned as much as I could while living on my paradise island, but I felt the real training ground for taking on such an epic expedition would have to be at home. North Wales, with its large mountains, difficult terrain and very unpredictable weather, would prove to be one of the best places to prepare me. Moving back in with my parents would be no easy feat. Although they were pretty chilled characters, both my parents and I knew this could be challenging and stifling after the lifestyle I'd been living. As much as they would all be thrilled to have me home, especially my sister Tash, and Brodey who was now eight, it was important I didn't lose sight of my goal and dilute this dream of mine.

I made plans to fly home before the New Year and meet Rob in London. At the Royal Geographic Society, I would look at the best quality maps of Mongolia with him, look at routes, water points and talk in much more detail. Rob became my expedition manager and it was fantastic to have him on board. He knew Mongolia very well, had lived there for five years on and off; he had travelled all over the country and had a team including interpreters and fixers. This helped to move things along faster.

I'd been advised to take a chance and publicise my expedition like never before, despite the big risk of failure. This was a difficult one, and the dangers kept flooding into my head – especially at night when things seem a lot worse, I would be up for a few hours, thinking over the journey and the risks involved. I woke up one night after a nightmare in which I was alone in my tent in the wild on an incredibly windy night, holding my knife close to my chest, sweating and shaking as a pack of wolves circled, howling at the midnight sky. It wasn't the most pleasant of dreams! I had to block these thoughts out. I knew there would be times when doubts crept in. But daytime would come and I'd be planning like a mad man, feeling more focused and determined than ever before.

So I went for it and publicised the expedition everywhere. A friend I'd met in Thailand put me in contact with someone who created a fantastic website for me. Someone else created a logo. I began contacting companies for potential sponsorship – many said no, but many said yes, and by the time I arrived home, I had boxes sent from various suppliers waiting for me.

My uncle Felix offered to help fund the expedition and also

provided me with camera gear to shoot footage; I'd always self-filmed my adventures, and this one was particularly important. His support was hugely appreciated. I could then stop relying on the possibility of a National Geographic grant, as I needed to know as soon as possible what was happening with funding. Now that I was back home, and had some sponsors on board, the funds for the expedition, and Rob as logistics manager, we could take things further and look into dates, visas, routes, vaccinations, the trailer, gear and electronic equipment.

Naturally, I also needed to prepare myself physically. I had a multi-gym in my garage, and my uncle Luke had dropped off a tractor tyre and I spent three hours a day training harder than ever before, no matter what the weather was, in the dead of winter – it was pretty grim, but I didn't care. I was beating the tractor tyre with a sledge hammer, flipping the tyre, still working on my Muay Thai, doing body weight exercises, pull-ups, sit-ups and press-ups plus weights, trying to build my inner-core strength as much as possible, to be able to pull a heavy load behind me over a great distance and over mountains. I cycled and jogged with heavy rucksacks.

I covered almost everything and I had never felt as strong. I'm not the biggest of guys and if I trained for bulk, I would have burnt out fast when I was out there. I needed to maintain good weight, but muscle weight more than anything, as well as maintaining great agility, balance and all-round strength.

Now that I was in the UK and meeting people who had been to Mongolia, many more said they didn't think it was physically possible to walk across the country, especially alone. Some of them had ridden 1,000km across the country on horseback, while I'd never even been there at this point. It was pretty demoralising, but I was thankful for their honesty. In a way, this motivated me even more; I knew it would be a great thought for when I was struggling out there. I would look back and remember their words to help push me on.

I got the map out and asked Rob: which one of these days is the day that I could fail, which is the impossible day? People had done much bigger and better things and succeeded, so if I broke everything down into what was needed, it should be achievable. As long as I had food, water and the strength to continue, then I could battle my way through each day. Water points were the most important, and I would need to make sure I was carrying enough water on my trailer in between the confirmed water points.

A family friend, Paul, said he would build a wheeled trailer to suit my needs. It would effectively be my life support; it would be carrying everything I needed to make the trip a success, all my provisions, weighing up to a whopping 18 stone. I sent him a few other designs for him to work from, but again we were on a tight budget. We went for mild steel and I was provided with puncture-proof tyres, custom made. It's always important to have people on board who believe in what you're doing, and who listen and adapt to what's needed. Paul was great; we kept in regular contact and he would send photos of his progress.

I needed to test the gear, clothing and boots sent to me by sponsors, so my friend Martyn and I went for a walk across Wales, from south to north in the dead of winter. Cold, wet and rainy, it made for great training and was an enjoyable adventure across our home country – we got lost many times! I then went to visit Manuel Huber in Germany, and did a short solo trek in the Austrian Alps, which was great except for one nasty moment where I was almost taken out by a landslide. I tried not to think how I'd fare in Mongolia. When everything seemed in place, I went for a test run in Scotland, along the West Highland Way, with my trailer and all my gear in place. It was extremely stormy. I didn't get any sleep; I was freezing and had to cross so many rivers, waist high, requiring me to dismantle the whole trailer and take everything across piece by piece, while winds were gusting and rain lashing down. The next day the main board on my trailer where all my gear would lie flew off into the loch and everything started to get soaked. I had to call it off, get picked up and return home to Wales. It was pretty disheartening. But it was a valuable practice run, and I now knew what more I needed to do to get my gear ready.

Time was passing fast, and there were ups and downs, but everything was coming together. My main worry was that I only had a 90-day visa to cover 1,500 miles, pulling about 120kg over mountains and deserts – it didn't seem realistic. I had visions of being only one week away from the finish line, and being picked up. I could just switch the sat phone off so they couldn't find me – but I was never going to do that, as it could cause problems for the team who had sponsored my visa. I just had to hope I could get a longer visa once I arrived in the country.

Fourteen months had gone by since the idea had first popped into my head. During the last week before leaving I felt weird, with mixed emotions; as much as I felt ready, I would also question myself. I told myself it was normal. I had never tested myself in this way before. I told myself I had to rise to the challenge.

Somewhat fearful of the situations I might find myself in, I did a long voice memo to myself, a recording that I could turn to later, full of motivational words. I said: "You're out in the Gobi Desert now, you're facing great difficulty – keep going… There's nothing back here for you if you were to return and fail, so keep pushing forward…" When I was at my lowest point, I'd get that voice memo out in the hope that I could be motivated by positive words from the Ash Dykes who was at home with a full stomach, hydrated, and healthy. Hopefully, at whatever point that happened, it would help me to push on and continue.

Everything had been flown over ahead of me a couple of weeks in advance: the trailer, the five and a half weeks' worth of ration packs, stove, sleeping gear and clothing, everything except one rucksack which I would take with me. A Mongolian guy named Jenya had confirmed he would pick up the gear from the airport when it arrived.

I said my goodbyes to family and friends, put a video up on my social media for those following my exploits, packed everything ready to leave the following morning and got an early night. My parents were anxious, but excited for me.

I woke up early on 14th May 2014. My mum made me a bacon sandwich and I hugged her goodbye. She looked upset but remained brave as she knew I had to stay sharp. My dad could see how focused I was and added to this in his positive way, breaking it down step by step with me while driving me to the airport. He maintained a brave face also, and as we hugged each other I whispered to him, "I've got this," walked off and turned around to give him a big wave and smile as I walked through the departure gates.

***

Mongolia is sandwiched between Russia to the north and China to the south; sometimes seen as the heart of Asia, it's the second-largest landlocked country in the world after Kazakhstan, its next-door neighbour to the west. In 2014, Mongolia had a total population of less than three million, most of them resident in the capital city of Ulaanbataar, and from above it was like nothing I'd ever seen before. Although it has an ancient history, modern buildings dominated – yet beyond the city limits, low hills took over and stretched off into the distance, with the circular white tops of *gers*, traditional dwellings of the nomads, scattered on the smooth green land.

It was beautiful, and reminded me of something from *The Lord of The Rings*. The day I arrived it was sunny and bright, and the city was busy yet smaller than I expected. It wasn't as loud as other cities I'd been to, but the traffic was crazy and among the smells of sewage and pollution were waves of fresh air blowing in from the nearby countryside.

It was great meeting Jenya for the first time. He came up to me with a smile and shook my hand, saying, "Hey, Ash." He was lightly tanned, stockier and smaller than me by a few inches, with dark hair and dark eyes. We instantly connected and he made me feel welcome, showing me around and educating me in the local ways. He was excited about my expedition, telling me I was crazy as he laughed and looked out of the window, while driving me around. We laughed together as I looked over to the hills around the city, thinking to myself it certainly would be crazy.

Jenya had already booked me a guest house, but just before arriving there, we stopped by to check my luggage. Because Mongolia's so empty, on my trailer I needed to carry clothing to protect me from the extreme weather, camera kit, water, five and a half weeks' worth of ration packs, sleeping and cooking equipment. It was being taken away by what looked like a rusty old bus all the way to Olgii, where I'd see it next. We signed some paperwork, paid the cash and hoped for the best.

The guest house was perfect with a small kitchen, a communal lounge and bathroom, and a bedroom which was small but had everything I needed. I went back out with Jenya to meet his wife Ogi, who was also helping with the logistics. She had just suffered a car crash in her brand new car, and was fuming. I felt for her, especially because it was the other driver's fault. She politely greeted me before entering back into an argument with the driver and a few other observers. People in general, though, came across as friendly – Jenya was introducing me to different characters and I'd got a great impression of all of them.

After hearing that evening of my worry about the visa situation, the next morning Ogi picked me up from the guest house and took me to a visa office where she managed to get an extra 30 days. It felt like a huge weight off my shoulders – and now there were no excuses for failing. Ogi then wanted to take me to Gandantegchinlen, a Chinese-style Tibetan Buddhist monastery whose name translates as "Great Place of Complete Joy". Ogi and I circled the building and she turned the prayer wheels, perhaps praying for my safety. She knew her land and how unforgiving it was.

Jenya and Ogi took me about 50km out of the city to a beautiful green valley with pine trees, to learn how to enter a Mongolian *ger* respectfully. I'd have to do this often on my expedition, and it was important I didn't offend anyone along the way. *Gers,* like the yurts of central Asia, are traditional Mongolian homes made up of a simple circular frame covered with wool felt; designed by the nomadic people, they are solid to withstand the elements, yet collapsible and moveable.

As you enter, there is a step which it's rude to stand on – you have to step over it – and there is a coil of hedgehog skin hanging on the door frame, which keeps bad spirits from entering, and you must avoid knocking this. There are also two poles in the centre of the *ger* that you have to walk around instead of between; the ladies' section is on the right with the kitchen and the men's on the left, but it is acceptable to cross sides. When you're sitting, it's considered disrespectful to have your legs sprawled out, taking up a lot of room, so instead you should sit with your legs crossed or tucked in. You should accept a plate of food or drink either with both hands or with one hand whilst the other one touches your elbow.

Also, to further my cultural education, I was taken to ride the small Mongolian horses. The horse knew I was a beginner and took full advantage. I lasted five minutes before it got too risky. I didn't want to injure myself before I set out. And at the Chinggis

Khan museum, I learned that the locals get annoyed if you call him Genghis Khan, as that's what the Russians called him. Originally named Temujin, he was born around 1162 into a land where kidnapping, stealing and fighting among clans was pretty rife, and by 1205 he had got rid of most of his rivals, organised an army and called himself Chinggis Khan, meaning "ruler of all". By the time he died in 1227, his empire covered an area about the size of Africa.

When plotting my route, I wanted to take in the Altai Mountains, the Gobi Desert and the steppe. But Rob said I couldn't get too close to the border as it could be quite sensitive – the west borders Kazakhstan, Russia and China – so it was decided that I'd travel from the westernmost city to the easternmost city. From there we started looking at water points, because not being able to find water was the biggest threat; food points too, of course, as I couldn't carry enough rations for the whole trip. It would be cold in the Altai Mountains, then extremely hot in the Gobi Desert in the summer, exceeding 40°C. The predicted time for achieving the journey was 100 days.

My starting point was to be Olgii, a three-hour flight away in a small plane that would have to refuel as we crossed three quarters of the country. As we waited at the airport and I asked Jenya questions, I felt strange inside, ready but nervous. Then Jenya asked me all about Muay Thai, and all of a sudden while talking about training and fitness, my attention shifted from the worrying task ahead. I felt re-motivated; it was a reminder as to why I was here.

Yet on the flight, I again felt daunted as I looked down at the vast, empty wilderness. I knew it was sparsely populated but until I saw it, I hadn't imagined how extreme it actually was. The further we got from the city, the fewer and fewer communities there were; eventually I began to see just one *ger,* a small white dot on the ground, every few minutes or so. The terrain looked rugged and cold, and I remember thinking, *man, it's going to be lonely.* It was wild, deserted, and I wondered about wolves. The flight seemed to go on forever and thought about how much terrain I had to cover on foot. I now began to feel naive, a 23-year-old arriving in this country for the first time and telling people I was going to walk the entire length of it. I had big doubts. I saw myself as arrogant for thinking I could do such a thing. *Who do I think I am?* I felt out of my depth.

Arriving in Olgii jolted me out of this mood and back into excitement mode. It is a small, low-rise city high on a plateau in the middle of the Altai Mountains, with a river running through it. Beyond the buildings was a pale-brown land that stretched to the foothills, and the ridges beyond had a light dusting of snow. Eagles circled above: Olgii is famous for its Golden Eagle festival and traditional hunting with eagles. Close to the western border, it's a very Kazakh-influenced area with several mosques. It was dark, cloudy and cold, a hailstorm beginning. I was still nervous, but there was no backing out now. Everyone knew what I was planning. I had to get the jobs done and get ready to leave.

Until it was time to begin, I would stay with a guy named Agban, a highly respected mountaineer who picked me up at the airport. He was a tall Mongolian who made me feel instantly welcome in spite of the massive language barrier. I was used to such things by now after years of travelling and living in Asia; there is always a way to communicate, though you have to risk looking stupid in the process.

Night time came, and I stared out of the window from a small, warm and cosy hut, to cold, windy and snowy mountain peaks, with the moon gazing over from behind them. It was hard to deal with the negative thoughts in my head again that night. I had no one to talk to. I had put myself in this position. Maybe it was partly jetlag. I was expecting these feelings, though, and knew I had to block them out and fight through the negativity, to find the positivity again.

By the morning, the clouds had cleared and the sun was shining brightly. I was feeling much more positive, ready to get my stuff together and attempt the journey of a lifetime. We went to the market to buy some things I needed; I wanted colouring pens as presents for the kids I would come across along the way. The market – or bazaar – sold everything from horsemeat to Kazakh embroidery to construction equipment, and around the entrance was an area full of outdoor billiard tables. As Agban and I walked around the city, stopping to snack on mutton dumplings, everyone seemed to know him and shouted out to him, and he introduced me to everyone, so word spread like wildfire that I was about to attempt to walk across the country.

When we got back to his place, Agban, his nephew and I set up the trailer and tested it out. They started to wrestle and asked to see photos of me doing Muay Thai. At 10pm we went to the bath-house for a sauna. These places are common in Mongolia, I learned, as many people don't have hot showers in their homes.

As I was melting in the humidity I told myself to make the most of it, as out there in the mountains, I would be praying for that heat again. The intense heat of the sauna and scalding hot shower made me feel like a whole different person: it helped to clear and focus my mind as well as reset my body, allowing me go straight to sleep that night.

The day finally arrived. I woke up with a big nervous smile on my face.

# 5: The Altai Mountains – blizzards and sandstorms and dodging wolves

As I said goodbye to Agban, I knew I was going to spend a lot of time alone and even longer without seeing a familiar face again. All my previous adventures had been with a friend and I didn't know how I'd handle being alone. Agban, who had summited Everest in the past, looked worried for me, knowing the challenges ahead. We gave each other a hug and then went in different directions, as he walked back to the city and I headed off alone into the wild. This was my opportunity to see what I was made of. For now, I had to take it step by step, day by day, week by week and month by month.

I'd need to cover on average 15 miles a day to complete the expedition in 100 days, although often I'd have to walk much further to compensate for necessary days off. I was only roughly guessing mileage anyway. Leaving Olgii by road, there was a sign every kilometre, and I timed how long it took me to the next, and estimated from that – though I could always check in with my satellite phone to find out for certain. It should take me about three weeks to traverse the Altai Mountains. This vast range stretches into China, Russia and Kazakhstan, forming a natural border between Europe and Asia, and the Mongolian Altai are the highest peaks in the country, the only ones with permanent snow cover. The melting snow supplies lakes and rivers.

I set out from the city along a tarmac road, but there were few cars. The land around was unfenced, the scenery as ruggedly beautiful as I'd imagined with smooth sandy terrain reaching up into the rocky mountains. If I was going to come across wolves, it would be on this section. I passed maybe one person an hour, though that was busy compared with what was to come; it was lonely, but I just needed to find my routine.

I was still unsure how often to take a break, how long for, and how to judge the daylight hours: when to stop and pitch my tent, when to cook, when to wake up. Right now I was just seeing how my body coped with pulling 18 stone (120kg) behind me. I weighed 11 stone, so it was like pulling myself and a fairly big child, or a baby elephant. I'd never properly tested out the shoes I'd brought out with me either, but I try not to over-plan things, which can lead to stress; I'd rather just go out and see what happens, learn along the way. I reminded myself that they say it takes two weeks to break a habit, and I just needed to give it two weeks to blow off the dust and break into my wild side.

That night I pitched my tent right next to a lake, with a view of snow-capped mountains. The temperature was below freezing, too cold for me even to notice much about how my body was coping. I wrapped up warm from top to bottom and boiled some water for my ration pack, enjoyed the view and slipped in to dazed thoughts that this was actually happening. It got dark around 9.30pm but the noise of the wind and the flapping of the tent made it difficult to sleep; I tried listening to music through earplugs but that didn't work. Eventually I must have dropped off around 1am.

The next day I woke to a stunning view, feeling fresh, making breakfast and packing all the gear onto the trailer. The going was tougher on rocky terrain, into the mountains on difficult dirt tracks, but I was still full of energy when I reached a small settlement called Tolbo. I'd planned to stay there before the next big mountain pass, as I'd been told that would take all day. Instead, I filled up with water, while the local people came over to help and try out my trailer, then I continued.

With the training I'd done, I walked fast up a steep valley; it was tough, cold and getting windier the closer I got to the top, but the scenery was so different from anything I'd seen before – its main feature was its harsh emptiness – and I regularly stopped to take photos. The trailer took a huge beating as rock after rock constantly brought us both to a complete halt. It was getting late and I knew I'd have to find a flat area to pitch the tent soon – there was nowhere suitable so I'd have to keep powering upwards to the top of the pass.

As it began to get dark, I reached the top and found a flat field. I was pitching my tent in freezing, relentless wind and warming my hands every few minutes as I could feel frost nip setting in, when I saw a guy driving a motorbike towards me. I thought I was in the middle of nowhere, but there's always a local somewhere. As he approached, completely wrapped up in a long black gown, with a balaclava over his face, I realised he was just a young boy, curious about me and what I was doing. I shook his hand and cracked on with putting up the tent, and he stood happily watching me, whilst I struggled.

He waited until I'd succeeded in putting the last peg in the ground before he offered via hand gestures that I could stay at his hut in the distance, where smoke rose from the chimney. I wasted no time and accepted immediately, asking him another three times, just in case I'd misunderstood, then I packed up as fast as I could.

It was a concrete hut owned by a Kazakh family, who seemed happy to see me although I looked a mess – my face was red from the wind, battered by the extremes, but I felt so privileged to be here, I couldn't stop smiling and making funny gestures as I pointed out the window and gestured how cold it was. The family gave me everything; they fed me, gave me warmth, and let me wash myself – which involved standing in a small, metal baby bath as one of the boys poured warm kettle water over me, semi-naked with the whole family looking at me. I still couldn't stop smiling! They went outside to herd the livestock, so I joined in, and I loved seeing their life out here in the high mountains.

We then went back into the warmth, and had a feast of goat's cheese, yak meat and Kazakh *chai* (tea). As we relaxed, I showed them the piece of paper that Agban had done for me, which explained in Mongolian who I was and what I was doing. They were shocked.

The mother tried hard to talk to me, and though I didn't understand, it was better than being ignored, so I smiled back and did my best to answer. We exchanged hand gestures and understood each other well enough, and they tried teaching me the Mongolian words for the food and drinks they were giving me. I made the three kids happy by letting them watch a movie on my iPhone, then it was time for bed, though we were effectively all together in an open room. I found it hard breaking into the sleeping pattern, my mind would always wander, but this is all a part of finding my wild side.

And so another cold, sunny day began with the mother banging pots and pans. I had a filling breakfast and put my gear on the trailer. They didn't expect money, but I gave them a bit to show my appreciation. Just before I set off, I asked if there was a toilet around. The boy just pointed to the top of the hill full of livestock. I didn't hesitate but found it hilarious. I'd enjoyed my time with them and I was surprisingly upset when I had to leave, heading back into the extreme weather, not knowing if I'd come across a local family like that again, and knowing I had another day of lugging my heavy trailer up mountain passes.

I said goodbye to them all and plodded off, full of emotion. That day was difficult; I never cried on the expedition, but there were times that I was deeply upset for reasons that felt like a big deal at the time. But I was never sad or lonely for long; I'd get back into the swing of things and realise again why I was out here doing this.

The terrain was becoming more extreme. The winds were strong, so I wore a mask or wrapped my face in a scarf. The ground was icy, with rock-solid mud that brought the trailer to a halt, and I'd have to lean forward, dig my poles into the ground and pull with all my might. It was a workout in itself. The trailer wasn't just heavy, it was also pretty big and wide, with two bicycle wheels on either side, but I needed it as the kit was essential to my survival. Where the paths were strewn constantly with rocks, that would also throw the trailer about or bring it to a standstill, I couldn't be too rough, so as not to damage it. When I got it over one rock and it hit another straight away, it would drag my hips from side to side. The skin on my hips began to blister and it was painful. But I was making good progress, sometimes walking from 6am when it got light to 9pm when it began to get dark. On some days I would cover 50km, or just over 30 miles, over the course of 15 hours.

One long day, I had to cross a small river, followed by a wide frozen lake. I could see a few huts in the distance, and stayed focused. As I finally approached, the people invited me inside for *chai*; I couldn't resist and scrambled up the hill to their place. They were laid back, curious about me, and offered me a lot of food which I got down me as fast as I could, feeling super hungry. I sat resting with a full stomach feeling satisfied, and they drew pictures of a car and a motorbike to ask why I wasn't travelling like that. I laughed and tried explaining.

Just as I was about to leave, the man of the house seemed to be looking at me strangely, looking first at me and then at his wife. I didn't know what was going on. I was sitting on the bed and his wife was next to me breast-feeding her baby, with her husband opposite. The next moment he was pointing to both of us and moving his fingers together – using hand gestures to offer me his wife. I had no idea what to do, and whether this was a joke between them. I didn't want to offend but I started laughing, and thankfully they did too, eventually. I made a swift exit.

I was aware that there were wolves around, having come across paw prints of a healthy size. I met two nomads on horseback and one of them, in unmistakable gestures, told me there were wolves hunting up ahead and that I'd be eaten alive; he finished his mime with a look of terror. I laughed it off, pretty sure I'd be fine. Then I saw an eagle in the distance, hunting down its prey – an incredible sight. It reminded me that I was vulnerable, so I checked where my knife was, gripped my walking poles and got my music device out to take my mind off them. Wolves wouldn't risk hunting down a human, not with plenty of yak around – but who was I to say for sure, when a local told me otherwise?

The terrain was still extremely rocky, so each step was a lot of effort. I got rid of my bad temper by shouting back at a guard dog that started following me and barking. But when I occasionally ran into other people, it cheered me up no end.

One day I was getting up a good speed on a downwards slope but injured my shin, so I was looking for a place to pitch my tent when I was approached from behind by two motorbikes. They were Westerners, Pieter and Mandy, who were biking around Europe and Asia. It was a huge surprise to see them and a proper conversation felt great. We set up camp together and had a long chat before crashing out.

My first snow blizzard was not a serious one, but worrying: in a white-out of several metres I couldn't see where the track was leading, and although I had a compass, it disorientated me slightly, so I had to stay aware and alert. But as I walked on, the sun came out again and put me in a better mood, especially when the clear light revealed the beautiful sight of a valley opening up ahead.

Around day five, I put the first of the mountains behind me, and the rocky paths gave way gradually to sand. I was seeing a big change in myself as well as the landscape. I had my face wrapped up to protect me from the sun and sand. The day was hot and I enjoyed the sun and the moment, listening to music and stopping regularly to take in the view and get fluids down me.

I was still on what is considered the busy route in Mongolia, meaning a couple of cars a day, sometimes Westerners here for the mountain-climbing, and often locals would stop out of curiosity, take photos and try my trailer. A car full of guys pulled up and couldn't believe the distance I had already walked from Olgii, which made me feel good. One of the guys handed me a bracelet and told me that if I got into trouble, I should grip it, and repeat the name Allah.

The day of arriving in the city of Khovd was frustrating, as it seemed I could see it in the distance for hours and it wasn't getting any closer. It was small but a beautiful place to recharge myself and my equipment for a couple of days, and as I crossed the bridge into town, the wind blowing strong, I looked back to see a sandstorm. My contact in Khovd was Yanjaa and she and her family were so hospitable, offering me *chai* and calling me "Hero!", but for the first night I stayed in a guest house so I could unpack everything and crash out.

I felt on top of the world, my confidence back, looking forward to the next leg. I could see the road ahead leading up a hill out of the city and felt totally psyched up to leave. As I left Khovd two days later, Yanjaa cooked breakfast for me, her mum flicked milk on the cart and myself and prayed for me, and her husband showed me the route.

I walked fast and pushed myself to make the most of daylight hours, getting 50km under my belt that day as it was a good tarmac road. When I set up camp that night, near a *ger* beside a building site which I hoped might block the wind, I was surrounded by drunken men, looking in my bags and attempting to attach my trailer to a bus that was about to leave. I had to be firm with them as I was drained from the walk and just needed to eat and rest. Thankfully, the bus left without my trailer and with most of the drunks, though I still had to contend with a barking dog. Maybe I'd have to get used to camping in the wind.

Another night I planned to pitch on grassland near a small group of *gers*, but when I was waved on by an angry grandmother, I ended up surrounded by goats which did their best to munch on my snacks or my harness, and I had to chase them off.

I was surprised from my sleep another night by two teenage boys pulling up on their motorbike. When I unzipped the tent and said hello, I frightened them so much they stalled the bike.

The days were long, with the sun waking me up in the morning and keeping me warm until late evening. When I stopped for food at a roadside café, I'd just point at what someone else was eating and hope it came out the same.

I had planned to light camp fires to keep wolves at bay, but didn't see any trees for wood, and collecting animal dung to burn seemed more hassle than it was worth, so I tried to stay alert and know which pocket my knife was in.

Sometimes I didn't speak properly to anyone for two days, which was lonely; it was just something I'd have to get used to, part of the challenge I had set myself. Encounters with locals put a big smile on my face. As I passed some *gers*, watching out for the guard dogs, two guys chased me down on their motorbike. They wore long, colourful gowns and had wide, strong cheekbones. They offered me a *chai* to take away and tobacco to sniff.

Another day, as I admired the views of bright blue skies, bright green fields, the mountains in the distance, a group of locals came and lounged around the tent with me to learn about what I was doing. All of my stuff was laid outside and they could see that I had camera gear, solar panel, satellite phone etc, but I wasn't worried – I have always had a healthy respect for and trust in people.

When I asked locals how far it was to a place, they would give their opinion, but were usually way off, sometimes by 20 or 30 kilometres. It was funny, but would sometimes get me down. Other times I just prayed the next person I asked would give me the answer I wanted to hear.

At a garage in Darvi, I asked about a place to sleep. The man just laughed, but I stood blankly staring at him, hunched over after a long walk through rough terrain and sandstorms, and he realised I was serious. He showed me to a small guest house.

There I was greeted by three very polite and stunningly beautiful girls, and a drunk old man. When I passed him the letter explaining who I was and what I was doing, he pulled himself together a bit. The ladies gave me some *chai* and a really good, traditional Mongolian meal, a filling pasta-type dish with meat, carrot and potato, and they stared at me while I ate. The fact that they were so pretty and clean, while I was dirty, smelly, had a beard that had started to turn ginger and my lips were bleeding, made me ten times more uncomfortable. I offered them money for my meal, but they wouldn't accept it, saying, "You very nice, no money."

My body was taking a bit of a beating. I was suffering with blisters, and my lips were in a bad way due to the altitude and the cold and wind; they were dry, chapped and bleeding. Sometimes in the morning I'd drink my porridge from the bowl, and when I put it back down there'd be a flow of blood and pus. My lips were painful like that for a good two weeks. Sometimes the pain would wake me in the night.

Not long after passing Darvi, I went to stay at a small settlement in a beautiful green field surrounded by the Altai Mountains. My attention was drawn by one of the *gers* which had ropes across the top strapped to big boulders around the outside, to hold it down, while a solar panel on the roof supplied it with electricity. There was a wooden door and a chimney poking out of the top, and the straps that circled the felt were being put to secondary use as a washing line. As I set up my tent nearby, people came to greet me and all sat around – as fascinated by my home as I was by theirs.

We all tried to communicate using hand gestures and sometimes writing or drawing in my diary. Time flew by and as it was getting dark, about 10pm, they dispersed and I went inside. An hour or so later, I felt the tent go loose as if someone had pulled out a peg. I shouted, "Oi!" and unzipped the tent to see a guy running off in the distance. I thought maybe he'd come just to say hello and I'd scared him, and after checking the pegs were OK, I went back to sleep. The next morning, I woke to the now familiar sight of the sun shining brightly on brilliant green grassland full of livestock, with the Altai Mountains in the distance against the deep blue sky. I packed all of my gear – and noticed I was missing my solar panel.

When I thought about it, I realised that when I'd packed all my stuff in my tent, I hadn't seen it – he must have pushed it under my tent while we were all sitting around talking. This was one of the key parts of my equipment, needed to charge my satellite phone which helped identify where I was and track my whole route. It also helped to charge my camera, and of course I had committed to self-filming the whole expedition in return for being given camera equipment. So it was pretty vital, and I was devastated, and disappointed that I would now have to be less trusting.

Luckily, two days before I'd left, I had thought, *What if the solar panel breaks?* and as a backup I'd got a cable which would allow me to charge my main battery using either a motorbike battery or car battery, giving me power for two weeks. But it just reinforced how important it was to have a contingency plan.

I was upset about the loss. But it was up to me to rise above it and push on regardless. The challenge doesn't begin until something goes wrong. It's how you react that makes all the difference. I came across some construction lads again that I'd met a couple of days before, who tried to get the police to help. That didn't solve much but I appreciated the effort, and I appreciated even more when they said if I could walk 40km, I could stay at their construction site, charge all of my electronics and top up with water.

I blasted out the next kilometres, almost stepping on a venomous snake in my haste. I got there early and had a shower. After being in an extreme environment for close to two weeks, it was great being offered the luxuries of hot food and feeling clean again, and just to be around the guys and have a laugh, even though we didn't understand each other. I showed them photos of my country and family and of scuba diving, which fascinated them.

I slept in a *ger* and noticed how warm it was and how much noise it blocked out, and after a great night's sleep I ate a hearty breakfast of yak meat to send me off with a full belly and in high spirits. I reminded myself that the positives always outweigh the negatives and that most people were friendly and kind. I gave them one of my logo T-shirts, and we exchanged contact details since they were from the capital. Hanging out with those lads was such a morale-booster.

I now had only 250km to get to Altai. I set out on small tracks and two hours later I was watching eagles stalk their prey from above, enjoying the walk and the music on my headphones, when suddenly I was hit from behind by my first ever sandstorm. I was inside it before I knew it – dust flying, noise and darkness, the sand stinging my skin. I was only wearing shades so had to squeeze my eyes shut as I rummaged through the bags for my goggles, which would then allow me to search for my fleece. It was scary but exciting. I put my cap on, covered all my skin because of the whipping effect and the fact that a sandstorm also has small stones and pebbles. My lips were covered in Vaseline

Age 19, the beginning of my travels: China

On completion of our Cambodia/
Vietnam cycle

Learning how to survive in the
jungle with a Burmese hill tribe

We'd often do crazy things – like cliff jumping in Thailand

Trekking in the Himalayas

Muay Thai fighting in Thailand

Building up all-round strength and inner-core durability for Mongolia

Making my way out of the mountains – 'The Lonely Snow Leopard'

Taking on the Altai Mountains

Hospitable construction workers invite me inside

Fighting to stay alive in the Gobi Desert

A local nomad, appearing from out of nowhere

The beauty of the Steppe

World first – 1,500 miles, 78 days, solo and unsupported

Mi and me at the southernmost tip of Madagascar

Walking with friendly locals

The younger generation's first sighting of a *vasah* (white person)

Ring-tailed (catta) lemurs

The changing landscapes of Madagascar

Locals working the land with their zebu

Difficulty crossing rivers during the cyclone season

Making our way down the mountains

On Maramokotro – the highest
peak in Madagascar

World first – 1,600 miles, 155 days

but now the sand was sticking to them, and there was nothing I could do except wait out the storm. As my friend Manuel Huber would say, "You just have to learn to enjoy it!" And once it settled down about 30 minutes later, I was full of adrenaline, excited to have been through it and ready to push on.

I find when I'm walking long distances completely alone, thoughts from the past keep me going, and thoughts of what I'm doing and of the future help to motivate me. I started to think about my next expedition; not in a cocky way as I still wasn't sure I would complete this one, but as a way of inspiring myself to keep going, because if I could conquer this one, I could consider the next.

I started to notice neat piles of rocks and stone at the top of the highest hills. I was told by a local that this was a religious tradition, and that I should place a rock on each one and pray or make a wish. They were simple and austere, enclosed by wooden poles, yet beautiful and I had to take a photograph. Sometimes when the going was good, I just wanted to take it easy and enjoy the journey, and it was frustrating having to stop, take the trailer off, get the camera gear and tripod out, set it up, and start filming; then put the trailer back on, walk away for the camera to see; then take the trailer off again, run back for the camera, pack it up into the trailer again, put the trailer back on me and continue on my way... But it was important to record the unusual sights, for the outside world as well as for my own memories.

A group of locals who were driving past pulled over, having seen me previously near Olgii, and gave me horse meat and bread, which they said was the Kazakh national food. I wolfed it down instantly, and a massive vulture casting a shadow from above seemed to be waiting for the left overs. Once, as I was eating dinner by my tent, I saw camels in the distance. The terrain was transforming gradually from mountain to desert.

I was in the middle of nowhere: no vehicles, no people, no insects, not a breath of wind. I sat and listened for the faintest noise.

Jenya had said to me there's no such thing as silence. I never understood until that moment. It was so quiet, so peaceful, yet I could hear the slightest hum. For ten minutes or so I tried to figure out what it was. And then I thought: perhaps it was simply my own body functioning.

It was a tough pull up towards Altai, and I had to lean into both my poles and pull myself and the trailer up the slope, crouching over like an old man, the trailer dragging my hips from side to side. It was hot, and I was dripping with sweat and had to take in as much water as possible.

As I got higher, to 1,500 metres, it turned colder, and I came across a couple of dead camels, which felt quite eerie. I wondered how they had died, and if I were to die out here, would people pass me by like they did the camels? I made a massive 55km push to the city, with drunk guys in cars trying to grab my trailer in an effort to help – I had to try to communicate to them why I didn't want that. Car drivers were constantly stopping to talk and I just wanted to get there. Even the construction lads showed up and offered me vodka, and I had to decline, which you do by dipping your finger in the shot and flicking three times.

Finally, I arrived at Altai, where I would stock up for the next leg, try to let my lips and blisters heal, and eat and drink as much as I could lay my hands on. I was over the moon to have a day off. Over the last 17 days I'd walked through a snow blizzard and two extreme sandstorms, been told I'd be eaten by wolves and almost stood on a snake, I'd had my solar panel stolen and been offered a nomad's wife. I'd pulled my cart over some of the worst terrain imaginable. And this was just the beginning.

But I was surprised by my determination. After an easy day in Altai, waiting for my clothes to dry, I was raring to get going. I was always driven to achieve something I passionately wanted, but had never tested myself in this way. I realised I was ready to power on forward, and see how much I could take. I was excited to see what was coming next.

# 6: Surviving the Gobi Desert

Things were about to get a whole lot harder.

From Altai, I turned southeast in order to walk on dirt tracks. Pounding on a tarmac road was bringing back my shin injury from early in the walk, and I preferred the idea of smaller tracks, even if it meant entering the Gobi Desert earlier. The difficulty was that the water sources were unconfirmed, and Rob wasn't certain there was another for 250km, but I set out with 15 litres and was confident I'd find water to top up at settlements along the way. Rationing my water would in fact make me gradually but dangerously dehydrated over the next couple of weeks without me noticing it.

I was alone for such long stretches. For over two months in the Altai and the Gobi, I slept in my tent in the wilderness. I went over eight days at one point without seeing a single human.

On day 23 of the expedition, the weather was cool and cloudy. The puncture-proof tyres on my trailer were so thin, they were sinking in the soft sand. I had very little water left, and it was 35km to the next settlement. My feet were in agony. The blisters on my heels had been growing so much I'd had to burst them, disinfect them and tape them up. My kit included spare inner soles for my trainers, which had helped for a while, but now my heels felt as though they were on fire with pins sticking through them. Each step sent a shuddering pain up through my spine to my inner core. I had to walk on tiptoe, which in turn was causing my calves to seize up.

A man passing from the opposite direction stopped to see if I was OK. I smiled, told him I was fine and he offered me some dried banana. He said about two kilometres further on in the direction I was walking I'd find a place that had food, which motivated me. I walked for half an hour but couldn't see the place. I guessed he was wrong about the distance and I was in for a much longer walk.

I still had a beautiful view of the Altai Mountains, though I couldn't properly enjoy it. This was the most painful day I'd experienced so far on my adventures. A nomad approached on his motorbike, weaving all over the place. Clearly drunk, he toppled over and fell to the ground. When I reached him, he pointed to the bike and wanted me to lift it with him. We did, and he asked for a lighter for a smoke, still swaying. He was smaller than me but thick set and big boned – they all looked strong out here. He was friendly but I was desperate to get to that place with food and water. I could now see a *ger* in the distance, about an hour and a half's walk away. I limped on.

I made it at last to the little community, but I realised I'd pushed myself way too hard. I was delirious, suffering from heat exhaustion. I had to rest. I left my trailer and headed for the place that served food. Kids swarmed around me. I loved their freedom and sense of humour, but I had no strength and as they repeated my name and the same questions over and over, I let my head fall to the table with my arm curled around it. The locals saw I was in pain and told the kids to leave me alone; they brought me *chai*, then food. I couldn't even think of putting the trailer back on to find a place to camp, never mind the months ahead. I asked the waitress, using hand gestures, if there was anywhere to stay in the community. She went to talk to her friends. When she came back and said I could stay in her room just on the other side of the same building, I couldn't thank her enough.

Next day when I stood up, I expected pain but was astonished to feel good, physically and mentally healed by sleep. Over the moon, I gave the waitress 20,000 tughrik, about £7. I set off across harsh but beautiful terrain feeling absolutely buzzing, in full appreciation of feeling back to normal again. Lesson learnt: drink plenty of water, take your time, and don't push yourself too much.

While in that settlement the evening before, I had signal on my phone and received a call from Jenya. He said people in Ulaanbataar were now following my progress across the country, which made me happy.

"They've come up with a nickname for you too!"

"Er, OK, what's that?!"

"The Lonely Snow Leopard."

I loved it instantly. But I wanted to know why. I wondered if this was like calling someone a lone wolf.

"It's because the wolves have kept a respectful distance and haven't attacked you."

It was a great name – but at the same time slightly worrying because I couldn't help thinking "not yet". Still, the nickname gave me more motivation and inspiration for the journey ahead. The snow leopard, said Jenya, is the only beast to walk alone.

The hills rolled on and on ahead, the path zig-zagging from here to there. The terrain was tough going, soft sand and gravel, and the river crossings were playing on my mind. Before I came here, on the test run in Scotland, my trailer had started falling apart. I'd called an end to the demoralising test run and gone back to get the trailer rebuilt much stronger. But if anything went wrong out here, I had no backup, and no other way but to cross the river. When I made it to the next river, it was wide yet shallow, not too powerful. Drivers were washing their vehicles and I had a quick wash myself as I waded through.

I'd been looking forward to some warm weather, to feeling the sun on my face. But for the next week or so I faced unpredictable weather, from hailstorms to rainstorms to sandstorms. My chapped lips burned in the wind. The temperature could drop from 20 to below zero in the space of 20 minutes. It was intimidating to see a huge beast of a storm slowly making its way towards me: with heavy clouds pressing down and nothing but flat desert as far as the eye could see, I had nowhere to hide. Sometimes I'd see a long finger of lightning flash into the ground up ahead. I felt vulnerable, especially with my trailer being metal; it was even worse to hear a storm approaching at night. One night the worst storm I'd ever experienced struck, with such powerful winds that as I sat huddled in the tent, which was attached to my trailer, I had to hold on to the poles as the wind lifted the tent, pulling pegs out of the ground.

Sometimes I was lucky and the storm would drift past me as I walked. Other times the rain would drench me and cool me down, then the sun would dry me out. I sang out loud to myself, high on life, excited by the experience. Sometimes, I'd come across locals riding their short, sturdy horses, the men wearing the traditional dress of a long coat tied with a colourful sash, and a black narrow-brimmed hat. People driving by would occasionally stop and chat. One guy said he'd summited Everest but would never walk across Mongolia as it was too far. It made me feel great.

I told myself: *it's not about how much you can give, but more about how much you can take whilst still pushing forward. And no matter what happens, how low or negative you become, you have to ride through and continue to move forward. Quiet determination and the willpower to achieve it will lead you to succeed.*

The ground was flat and hard and rocky, and the skies blue and clear and bright: a vast, open landscape. I stopped at Jinst, which had just a few huts and *gers*, a couple of banks and a new-looking guest house with a red metal roof and a shop in the front. A hailstorm battered us that night and I listened to it from the comfort of a bed as I ate pretty much all of their supplies. Before I left again, the locals made sure I had enough water, which I collected from the well. They were so welcoming, it made me sad to leave. I pushed on, with the mountain ridge clear on the horizon in one direction, and desert sand dunes in the other.

Unfortunately the banks in Jinst had been small local ones and there was no way for me to use my bank card. Somehow I'd miscalculated how much money I'd need to carry with me, and I no longer had any cash to buy food along the way. I'd run out of snacks and was restricted to two ration packs daily, adding up to 1,600 calories – less than I ate while training at home, let alone walking all day pulling a heavy weight. I had breakfast when I got up around 6am, then would go 12 or 14 hours before my next bite to eat, so it got me pretty angry if the wind blew sand into the pot as I boiled water. I noticed myself losing weight fast. I was effectively starving myself.

I couldn't use too much of my water for making food, as I needed the water to drink. Here in the Gobi Desert, I had to stay focused and alert to make sure I had enough water the whole time. I made the most of any river crossing, topping up my bottles with their built-in filters. Once, some local people stopped – well dressed, two men and a woman, driving a truck – and although we couldn't understand one another they offered me drinks and biscuits that tasted like manna from heaven. It made my day that they were so kind and understanding.

One day I was excited to see a long train of camels walking past me through the empty, dry land dotted with meagre tufts of grass; these were two-humped Bactrian camels with thick and shaggy hair, unique to Central Asia. The weather was a mix of hot temperatures and hailstorms, but I gradually began to understand the weather a bit more and be prepared.

I had to be careful to follow the correct path, though; it was vital, because that path would lead me to the next water source – it was my lifeline – yet it was easier said than done. I got lost again and again as the paths split off in five or six different directions. How the locals managed, I don't know. I took a 20km diversion and had to turn back on myself. I was still making good progress, but the dehydration, the hunger, and the difficult navigation started to break me down mentally as well as physically. I covered my face with netting to keep off the flies and mosquitoes.

Guchin-Us was the halfway point in terms of mileage. Once I got there, that was half of the country covered. That spurred me on, chased at times by dogs and approached by curious horses. That night, I ended up being taken into someone's *ger*, where young girls giggled at me – I didn't mind as I knew I looked like a yeti and they made me laugh too, which came as a sweet relief of tension. After I explained to the older man that I had no money to pay for food or shelter, the girls also asked if they could pray for me; unfortunately, although this was nice, I felt so uncomfortable I struggled to control my laughter and my eyes were watering with it as they sat and whispered their prayers.

But from there I had to ration my food even more. It could be weeks before I reached a city with an ATM. I counted out exactly five salted peanuts every hour as a snack, and was tempted to take a third ration pack but couldn't risk running out. I was so hungry that I walked towards a *ger* and they invited me in and gave me three bowls of yoghurt. But it seemed like a bad idea the next morning. I dashed out of the tent stark naked and let loose with severe diarrhoea. I just had to laugh at myself (especially with wild camels watching), but of course the diarrhoea dehydrated me even more.

I'd been suffering from dehydration for two to three weeks, unbeknownst to me. It had crept up on me and I was slipping into heat exhaustion. My steel trailer felt like a concrete block as I dragged it through the sand; it was impossible to build up any momentum.

On day 42 of the expedition, I woke up feeling much worse, with a terrible headache, and in a lot of pain. My organs were crying out in agony for replenishment. After walking for just ten minutes, sweat was pouring off me. Every part of me ached and I'd lost a lot of weight. I knew I had to push on to the next settlement, where I could get fresh water and some nutrients down me, I hoped, and rest. So I continued. But it was near impossible. It took me five minutes to cover 100 metres, and then I'd have to rest. It was 40°C, with no breeze. I hid from the burning sun underneath my trailer since there was no natural shelter. My legs stuck out from underneath and felt like they were melting. In my delicate state, the gravel and stones dug into my back like nails. I forced a little water down, even though it was now hot and horrible.

I suddenly realised that this could be my impossible day: the day my expedition would fail. If I didn't get up from under the trailer, I could quite easily die out here in the Gobi Desert. It was too late for any backup plan, too late for any SOS call to summon help in time. I had to keep getting up and pushing on. It was down to me to make it to the settlement. I wanted to stay alive. But how difficult it felt.

I needed to break the problem down into manageable steps and goals, taking me back to that mind map. If I could make it to Delgerkhangai, four walking days away, I'd be safe. I needed something to get me past the impossibility. I recalled Ripley's phrase: "Incredible is the ability to continue no matter what."

Semi-delirious, I tried to picture "Incredible" as a person or thing in my head, to give myself something inspirational to follow. I imagined Incredible as a figure that would get out from under the trailer, and set itself tasks. Incredible was a god that pulled me out from under the trailer. Somehow I mustered the determination and strength to get myself to safety; crazy as it sounds now, that's how I survived.

A few days later I saw in the distance two *gers* which weren't on the map, in the middle of nowhere. Step by step, stubbing my feet on the stones as I could barely lift my legs, I made it to a tiny settlement. They saw I was in a bad way and invited me inside. I pretty much collapsed on the floor. They gave me water and milk. There was a couple with four children, all curious but they could tell I was in pain. The mother laid down a few blankets and a pillow, and gestured that I should sleep. They flipped back a section of the *ger* to create a breeze on my face, which helped me drift off to sleep. When I woke, still in pain but feeling better, the man asked if I wanted to stay, and they fed me yak meat and *chai*. I soaked up the experience of being with the nomads, the kids playing and the camels outside making crazy noises. Outside, beyond them, there was absolutely nothing as far as the eye could see.

I prepared for sleep, wrapping myself in a -40°C sleeping bag, wearing clothes and a woolly hat yet still shivering. I woke up the next morning feeling even worse, but I had to keep going. I thanked the family and left.

The paths were just as tough, the sun just as powerful, and I needed to stay focused. This final day's push to Delgerkhangai was probably the worst of all, twice as painful as the previous days. I could finally see a settlement up ahead but it never seemed to get any closer. It had everything I needed to survive but it remained far away on the horizon, taunting me. Still sipping at hot water, I dreamed of ice cold water and shade. When I finally got there it turned out to be a very small settlement, but I got a room and there was a shop with water and food. The people were welcoming, happy to let me rest. I felt like I'd been near death and I needed to recover properly.

For the next six days I stayed there. I had nightmares of roaming the desert with nothing, not even my trailer, crawling around searching for water. I could feel my insides turning to dust; I was screaming, and the next moment heading for a shop that served ice-cold milkshakes, to pour one over myself. They were mad dreams and I woke up feeling both good and bad. Good because I was safe now; bad because I knew I had to take on the desert again.

I couldn't bear walking to the shop in the sun, so I'd wait until the evening and have the wonderful local yak meat in a wrap, khuurshuur and dumplings. I drank a lot and since there were no healthy foods to buy, no fruit or vegetables, I took pills to help my system. I was dizzy and couldn't sleep well with the constant nightmares, getting hot and then cold, getting up to urinate – a dark orange colour. One day, I looked at myself in the mirror. I looked in pain, but said to myself:

"Sort yourself out, you're losing it – get your shit together."

Not very heroic words, but it worked. I needed to get my mind and body believing that I would be leaving again soon. I started preparing my kit, washing clothes and organising gear. I had a good wash and put on fresh clothes. One of the shops re-opened and had apples and mackerel, and I started stuffing my face with goodness. Food is medicine. I told myself that I'd recover and just had to take it day by day.

This incident had knocked my confidence a bit. If I hadn't found this settlement, would I have made it? It worried me. I had signal on my phone here and spoke with my parents; they were concerned, and my mum did her research and discovered that the recovery time from heat exhaustion is usually much faster, and that I was most probably on the borderline of heatstroke. But I was now recovering.

I also spoke to Rob, who recorded me on Skype to keep my followers updated. One of his questions was, "Have you thought about giving up?"

The truth was that it made me even more determined. Yes, I was more nervous, but I was more focused. Before I came to Mongolia, I knew this could potentially happen, I knew the risks involved; what I didn't know was how I would react if it did happen. I didn't know what my personal limit was. I didn't think I'd give up or call for help, but I couldn't be sure until it happened to me. When I heard my reply to Rob, I knew it was true that whatever stood in my way, I was determined not to quit, not to stop until I crossed the finish line.

The locals had looked after me so well that it was hard leaving after a week with them. I felt nervous about going back into the extremes on my own; fearful now of the sun and the swift damage it could cause. Having made a mistake with the route before, I took my time. I had to adapt to the conditions of this journey. I felt more experienced, as though I'd learned a necessary lesson.

Yet I was back to the same old sleeping bag, the same old tent, eating out of the same old plastic bag. I really felt the depths of loneliness. And it was difficult to get the motivation back.

The days were long and the hours seemed to go by slowly. I was walking up a hill on a sandy path for a long time one day and flies were constantly landing on my face. I wasted so much energy attempting to swat them away every ten seconds that it completely drained me and I flipped out. Usually that helps me to laugh at myself but this time I didn't.

But it gradually got better, the track hardened up so it was easier to pull the trailer, and best of all, it was only one more day to Mandalgovi. Before I'd set out, I'd said that if I made it there, I'd only have just under 500 miles left and would call it the finishing stretch – even though it was more than twice the length of my home country of Wales! On day 54 I arrived at Mandalgovi, which was a good milestone. But even more than that, once I reached a settlement near there, I'd have broken the previous world record for a solo and unsupported walk across Mongolia: 1,012 miles.

Sometimes it still felt like everything was stacked against me. I even ran out of my favourite ration pack, chicken tikka masala, and had to eat strawberry porridge for dinner! Then as I pushed on, I noticed the weather start to get cooler. Clouds felt like heaven after weeks of severe temperatures. Grey-brown sandy earth gave way to joyously bright yellow grassland. A rainbow reached down into a flooded plain. I was leaving the desert behind and breaking onto the steppe.

The Mongolian steppe is another empty land with no trees, but the golden-green grass cheered my spirits and re-motivated me. It was such a relief to have made it to this point. I soon had only 320 miles left to my end-point location of Choybalsan in the northeast corner of the country, close to the border where China meets Russia. I could see eagles hunting in the distance, and gazelles leaping over the long grass in the distance.

One night, I got out of my tent to get water. It was pitch black, and I looked up at the Milky Way and all the stars around me. Then as I turned to go back into the tent, I saw lights glimmering faintly in the distance. I just stood there frozen, dazed: it was the city that marked my finishing point.

The population was higher in this part of the country, and locals stopped to take photos or ask what I was doing. Sometimes they'd invite me over to share some lunch with them. It felt as though I was close to the end, though I had to stay alert and aware. There were thunderstorms and lightning, and the mosquitoes were relentless, and I had to watch out for snakes, too – I almost stood on the back of a big pit viper. But the walking wasn't too difficult and I was following a river so I didn't need to carry such a heavy load of water on my trailer. The last 200 miles were something special that will stay with me forever. I felt quite calm and concentrated, savouring the moment.

After 78 days I made it to Choybalsan, the easternmost city of Mongolia, becoming the first recorded person ever to walk the country's length, solo and unsupported. It was hilarious to notice that I'd sanded down the ends of both my walking poles by almost a foot over the 1,500 miles. And I'd gone through two pairs of footwear and a pair of Crocs. But I'd made it in one piece.

I'd slept in *gers* for a few nights, and had stayed in towns for eight to ten nights, but otherwise slept alone in the wild.

Suddenly, with me still looking like a yeti with a big red beard, I was on TV screens.

"Congratulations – you've achieved a world first. How does it feel?" asked the newsreader. "Mongolia World First" read the caption.

"It still feels so surreal," I answered, with a big smile on my face.

When I went out there, I wasn't sure how I would handle being alone, and facing all the physical challenges. It makes you realise just how capable we are as individuals. Mongolia had turned out to be an extraordinary country of breath-taking beauty. One thing that stayed with me was the immense hospitality of the Mongolians throughout, always giving, always wanting to help – an exceptionally warm and welcoming people. My many invites into remote *gers* would stay imprinted on me forever.

"And what's the next challenge?" asked the newsreader at the end of the interview.

"The next challenge… I can't reveal just yet unfortunately, but there is something in the pipeline – and it will be big."

This expedition had been a make or break for my future, as I knew from the outset. Its success and the coverage in big global press opened the door to other opportunities, and I hoped this would allow me to continue pursuing this passion I'd found: to travel across countries that I know little about, to experience the local ways of life, to challenge myself but also to share stories from those countries with others from the outside world.

And so after I returned to the UK in August 2014, there was little time to sit back, relax, and bore my friends with travel tales in the pub. I was already looking ahead to the next adventure, and in the meantime I certainly kept busy over the next months. I went on a speaking tour of theatres around the UK, talking about my adventures; this was organised via Speakers from the Edge, and it helped raise some money for me to live off. I also earned some money to cover my UK living expenses when I was featured in a short documentary on Discovery Channel's *Daily Planet,* which went out across North and South America, and was then sold on to Canada and finally worldwide; and on Channel 5's programme *Weather Terror: No Escape.* All of this, and then being invited to 10 Downing Street to meet the Prime Minister, helped to build publicity for my next adventure, as did winning the National Adventurer of the Year Award via public vote. By then I was deep into planning the next expedition, which the UK national media were keen for me to announce. But I needed to find sponsorship to make it happen.

With all the publicity, I'd hoped the search for sponsors would be easier but it was extremely tough nonetheless. When I announced the next expedition, I still didn't have the money to make it happen.

In the meantime, though, I'd achieved what I'd set out to do. I don't know if I'd have been able to walk solo and unsupported across Mongolia if I hadn't done everything that came before, building up those track habits and experience, which all made for a powerful force that helped me survive. Stubbornness had helped me too. I didn't want to come back, and have people clap me on the shoulder saying, "At least you tried your best." I had to do it because I'd told everyone. I knew the challenges would come close to breaking me, but I believe it's about how you face everything. It was up to me to deal with the difficult times positively or negatively. That's the difference between succeeding and failing. It's about shining when you're only glowing. Pushing on through.

A lot of people had told me that this expedition was impossible. But it doesn't matter if they don't see it for you. It's important that you see it for yourself. You must mentally believe it before you physically go on to achieve it. And so I had to believe the next one would happen too, and keep going with my plans.

# Part Three:
# TRAVERSING
# MADAGASCAR

# My route across Madagascar

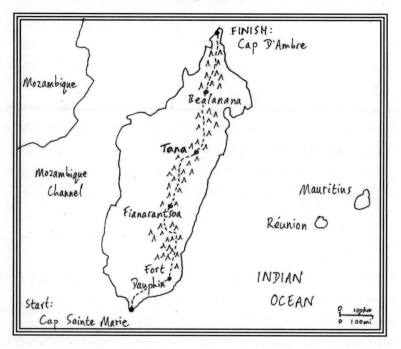

# 7: Cap Sainte Marie: Another desert, and news of civil unrest

I stood at Cap Sainte Marie, the southernmost tip of Madagascar where the Indian Ocean meets the Mozambique Channel. The wind was blowing off the ocean, a cool, salty breeze. I was about to set off on another journey that had never been completed before: to walk the entire length of Madagascar...some 1,600 miles, over five months. My goal was to take on the eight highest mountain summits, as well as the densest jungles, through the heart of the fourth largest island in the world.

It was in Mongolia in 2014 that I began thinking about where I would head to next; it helped to motivate me and keep pushing me forward. The people I met along the way there were so hospitable that I thought I'd like to traverse a country where I would constantly come across locals and could get to know the people, understand their way of life and see how they survive in extreme and often remote locations. Madagascar in 2015 had a population of around 24 million, over 20 million higher than Mongolia in a country a third of the latter's size, so I'd be engaging with people much more regularly. With 80 per cent of its plant life and wildlife found nowhere else on earth, I knew that this would be a very different experience. I found a logistics manager, Gilles Gautier, founder of Madamax, who'd spent over 30 years leading teams from the likes of *National Geographic* around Madagascar. He told me about the mountain ridge lying east of the centre and running almost the entire length of the island.

"It's asking to be walked," he said, adding that there was no evidence to suggest that anybody had ever walked the island through the interior following the plateau. This got me excited. It was the desire to explore an unfamiliar land that drove me, as well as the need to push myself. There would be sections in the interior with no tracks whatsoever, according to Gilles, where I'd just have to thrash through the jungle.

I'd done a reconnaissance trip to see the kind of thing I'd be up against. Hacking through the jungle was hard. You couldn't move too fast and you had to be aware, on the lookout for snakes and spiders. There would be sections with no-one around. "Malagasy don't go to the big mountains," said Gilles. "They'd freeze to death!" I'd seen that it would be difficult to find a good route up the peaks; some were like sheer pyramids of rock. It wouldn't be walking, it would be scrambling with hands and feet.

Back at home, I'd been training three hours every day, in my back garden and garage; Muay Thai on a bag; a tractor tyre which I flipped and beat with a sledge hammer to build up my inner core, and a lot of body weight exercises, as I believe this builds everything – strength, flexibility, agility, balance, coordination, speed and power. These workouts were exhausting, but by training physically, I was also training mentally. Especially on cold and rainy mornings when I lacked motivation, I tried my best to be disciplined and throw myself out there regardless.

It was only four weeks before I left that I found the funds to make it happen. I was sponsored by my local county, Conwy, as well as a handful of businesses who felt inspired to team up with me for this journey. With the generosity of these people, I gathered together £9,000 to put towards the expedition and get it off the ground. It wasn't all that much when you took into account the flights (first to Madagascar, and then an internal flight to the south), insurance, visa, vaccinations, equipment, guides and living expenses whilst out there for four months. I'd have to fund the rest of it myself but this was a big boost, and I'd just have to be careful with what I spent.

On 4th September 2015 I set off from home: a couple of hours on the plane to Paris and then a 10.5-hour straight flight to Antananarivo, the capital city of Madagascar. It was only in the last hour of the flight that I realised I wasn't thinking much about the expedition. Was I just getting used to taking a plane to remote locations? Or was I choosing to ignore my emotions, so I didn't worry about the pain ahead? Yet I was upbeat and keen to get started. I was in peak condition, full of energy and raring to go. It was a beautiful country and I felt ready.

I believe we're born with two things: roots and wings. Roots to know where you come from, and wings so you can soar to different parts of the world. And it's a shame not to explore this world we live in. For the next few months I'd be plunged into the world of the Malagasy people, and I'd have to adapt to the rhythm of life in small communities where people had few resources and lived off the land. The culture would change as I crossed the country, Gilles had said, and would be different from anything I'd experienced before. The coastal tribes were from Africa while the central island tribes were Asian. The Malagasy say Madagascar was once joined to India and Africa, and that those two continents split away leaving the island of Madagascar. I'd be going from grassland and savannah to tropical rainforest and tropical dry forest. It would be constantly changing.

The main airport for the capital of Madagascar was just big enough to accommodate one plane – they don't schedule two flights at the same time as the airport's too small. I'd be back there in a few days to fly to a city in the south of the island, then drive from there to the southernmost point. Meanwhile, a government official arranged a letter of invitation, giving me five and a half months to complete the expedition.

When we went to get the visa stamped, they were quite amazed by what I was planning to do, and stamped six and a half months to allow "for the times that you might get ill or injured". I'd already accounted for that, but having a whole extra month was fantastic and took a bit of pressure off. I'd organised my expedition so I'd be setting out in the cool and dry season, but it also got dark early – at half six it was pitch black; there wouldn't be a lot of daylight hours to walk in at first, but I was in no great rush, with six and a half months stamped into my visa.

I'd arranged to have a local guide with me on this journey. I'd still be supporting myself, but since I'd be coming across local people much more often in Madagascar than I had in Mongolia, it seemed a shame not to be able to learn their stories and communicate with them. Having a translator would help me to understand the people and share stories with the outside world. I wouldn't have the same guide throughout – different guides would cover different sections. To have done the journey solo through the mountains would have been more reckless and I was grateful for their help, and liked the idea of working through the challenges alongside a local.

I started to look for a local SIM card I could take out into the wild with me to provide me with 3G signal, as there was reasonable network and connectivity to the internet even in some remote locations in Madagascar. Any chance I had, I wanted to post online, to keep everyone updated back at home and in the rest of the world.

It was a busy first day, but we got a lot of stuff done so I went to get a pint of beer and a steak with one of the guides, Joe, at a little shack – the entrance was just covered by beads and I'd never have found it myself, but it was nice. I got back to my room feeling happy with the day; then there was a power cut so I just hit the deck for a good night's sleep.

Then the next day started with an email from Gilles saying that there'd been an uprising and conflict between the cattle thieves, or bandits, and the army in the south. It had resulted in a few dead and injured military personnel, and it was quite a scary place to be right now. Of course, that was exactly where I was heading. I went through my map work with Joe. I would be pretty much walking right into the area of the conflict, just north of Fort-Dauphin. But I'd start down at Cap Sainte Marie and it would take me another two weeks or so to walk back up there, so hopefully it would have calmed down a bit by then. I didn't want to change the route I had planned, if possible.

We went to the top of Antananarivo, over 1,200 metres above sea level; down below had once been forest, lakes, lush green land, but the city had expanded and now there was no forest, and the lakes were polluted. I then had a meet and greet session with the press, and met Jonah from the Lemur Conservation Network. I hoped to meet him again up north towards the end of my trip, to search for a lemur that's one of the rarest primates in the world. It is native to Madagascar and there are only about 50 left. If the deforestation and hunting continue, they'll be extinct in about 20–25 years. So he was doing important work.

Stopping for a beer with a few guys and girls afterwards, I met a girl from the south who said it was a dangerous area; relatives of hers had been shot and killed. Obviously that left me worried. The last thing I wanted was for the bandits to be pointing their guns at me. To them I was nothing, just another human life, which to them wasn't a lot. Possibly the best route would be completely off the track, hacking my way through the dense jungle and bush to hide. I wouldn't have as much access to food, but I'd have my ration packs and as long as there was water along the way, maybe I could stay away from them. It made me nervous. I had to be vigilant.

I dozed on and off during the flight to the south. When I looked out of the window, the scene below was covered in cloud, which was perhaps just as well, as I didn't have to see the rugged terrain that I would be up against. Two to three minutes on the plane equalled a whole day's walk. An hour and 45 minutes later, I arrived at Fort-Dauphin on the southeast coast and was greeted by Mi (pronounced "me"), the Malagasy guide who would be trekking with me for the first section. He looked about 18 years old, but was actually 34. He had a good sense of humour and it was great to have him on board.

Mi said he was going to go home and sleep for a few hours, because he'd had a rough ride and the car broke down. I was expecting him to come back refreshed, ready for us to go through the water points together, map our route, pack our gear and make sure we had enough food; we needed to check what each of us was carrying. Instead, he rocked up completely drunk. He went to wash his hands, turned the tap on and couldn't even see where the water was running – how did he get drunk so fast?! I'd been warned by Joe to make sure that Mi didn't drink, and now I understood why. I sent him home and told him to come back at a certain time, but he didn't.

I tend to be quite a laid-back person, but I was pretty angry and disappointed. You don't drink when you're heading out on a week-long trek to the next sign of civilisation – alcohol dehydrates you and we'd be trekking through a desert. This was too big an expedition for second chances. I'd have to crack on, and I called Gilles and arranged for Joe to meet me back here in a week, so I only had to rely on Mi for seven days. This was one problem I didn't need – I was already worried enough about the small war that was going on.

The next morning, Mi arrived late, but we got some breakfast. I went to the ATM, hoping it wouldn't swallow my card as had happened once before – thankfully it was fine. I was travelling, as always, on a tight budget; still, it had a tendency to make things more adventurous and extreme. Unfortunately, I had to hire a 4x4 to drive down to Cap Sainte Marie, which was costing me 700,000 Malagasy ariary, about £120–140: that was a huge bite into the budget, but the price was fair since it would take eight hours, and then the driver had to stay the night and drive back.

It turned out Cap Sainte Marie was actually a national park, and was closed. After a lot of talking and negotiating I had to pay for a security guard, a second guide and a ticket to allow me to walk back through the national park. It felt a little excessive having all those chaperones but it was only 32,000 ariary, a few quid, and I didn't have a choice. We drove the final 12km to the coast through the fading light with cheery traditional Malagasy music playing in the car, windows open. We stopped at a lighthouse where they let us stay in a couple of empty rooms.

At dawn I was excited to be checking water supplies and packing up for day one of traversing Madagascar. All the locals were looking at the size of my bag, tutting.

"Heavy, heavy!"

*I know…* I thought. But I had everything I needed: two pairs of footwear (heavy boots and sandals), ration packs, stove, water, electronics and chargers, a solar panel and clothes. It added up to a heavy weight.

Soon I was looking out over the Mozambique Channel and the Indian Ocean. Directly south from here was Antarctica. North was 1,800 miles of jungle, desert, savannah, tropical dry forest, tribal communities – and who knew what else? I was anxious but excited. Rocks tumbling around us, we scrambled a hundred metres down a steep mountain path to the bottom, where I touched the ocean. Then off we went.

There were no paths, just sand dunes separating desert from beach, and we simply followed the coast. Walking in the sand proved difficult; it was hot, too, and I was still wearing trousers and a shirt which suddenly seemed wrong when I'd be walking down a beach for the next few days. I felt the weight of my rucksack – I was already regretting bringing so much. But I loved the quiet and emptiness and the stunningly beautiful beach, bright sand and big waves. We saw eggshells of the enormous elephant birds that became extinct centuries ago. Every two or three hundred metres we'd come across an almost naked man fishing with a long bamboo stick, to take food back for his family.

As we made our way beyond Cap Sainte Marie, the security guard and the second guide turned around, and Mi and I went on alone. After an hour or two of trudging in 40-degree sun with a heavy pack, parched, the sweat pouring off us, we paused to take a breather, collapsing on burning sand. I was watching a spear fisherman in the crystal-clear shallows when all of a sudden, farther out, a humpback whale launched itself out of the ocean. "Amazing!" I said to Mi. He laughed. To see that on day one seemed a good omen.

We could see some sort of village up ahead, but it was starting to get dark, and my feet were sinking two to three inches into the sand, so each step was pretty agonising. But I was still in high spirits. It turned pitch black and we kept aiming for the fire glowing in the distance. Eventually we found a small community

– it seemed to have started off with just a single family but the word spread, and as I set up my tent I was surrounded by people from the young kids to the grandparents, all curious and amused by this Westerner lugging a rucksack around, happy just sitting and watching.

It was quite a special moment but I was too tired to appreciate it. Mi cooked up a good meal of rice and noodles. We'd walked about ten hours, covered maybe 20km (13 or 14 miles) in the sand. When I got back to Fort-Dauphin, I'd need to lighten my load, get rid of a lot of stuff – I couldn't do another 120 or more days like that one. In the tent, I went through the evening routine: changing the SD card in my camera, doing the audio log, making sure everything was ready for the next day.

It was hot when we packed up to leave around seven the next morning, but I felt rested, and there was a cool breeze blowing off the ocean as we walked along this incredible, huge strip of beach. It was hard to walk in the sand with the weight of the rucksack, my feet sinking. But I had wanted a tough challenge! We took regular stops to make sure we got our intake of water. My bag pulled down on my shoulders and I strapped it hard around my waist – like a rock-solid clamp – but it began to rub. I gave my hips a break by applying the pressure on my shoulders again. These first days were painful, but day by day I knew I'd feel stronger. I found that adapting to different situations or terrains was one of my strengths.

The sun was beaming down, and a traditional Malagasy fishing boat came into view with its sail up. The fishermen came ashore, and were friendly. A few laughed and were quite bolshy and loud, saying, "English!" But the rest shook my hand, saying, "Salaam," hello. We eventually made it to a village with seven or eight huts and a kind of restaurant, where they cooked us zebu steak – zebu are the local humped cattle, found all over the country – and rice with tomatoes and onions, and then papaya for dessert, which was heavenly. It was great to rest our stiff, aching muscles. When we decided, a couple of kilometres on, to pitch our tents before it started to get dark, we were surprised to hear people calling out to us from the top of a sand dune.

Amazingly, a family were up there, a husband and wife and three children, living in one tiny hut on top of a sand dune surrounded by cactus that acted as a wind-break. There was a sandy patch just big enough for our tents. The people were hospitable and friendly but not pushy. They give us rice and fish. The water they drank was from the sea, filtered into a well, so it was salty but they'd adapted to that meagre way of life in extreme conditions. Their days revolved around fishing in the ocean, and selling fish in the "common village" (a place that might have a generator for electricity, and a weekly market) in return for rice, and collecting water from the well. They got by with these bare rations – rice, salt water, fish – and they lived on the dunes. It was survival at its rawest, and it was an incredible experience to get up close and personal to it.

People were generally happy to see us in this remote region, where there were very few people around. The next night, we found a village in the middle of absolutely nowhere, and as Mi went to get permission for us to camp there from the sheriff and I sat waiting, looking after the rucksacks, before I knew it I was again surrounded by Malagasy of all ages. For the younger generation, it was possibly the first time they had ever seen a white person. We went to pitch our tents and as I turned on my stove, the stove that got me 78 days across Mongolia, it broke. Thankfully we could go back to the village and ask for firewood so we could start a fire and cook – having skipped lunch and gone almost 12 hours with no food, the noodles tasted heavenly.

I woke up to a baby crying, and rain. We huddled under a little wooden hut to say goodbye, *"Valooma"*, and off we went for another day's trek. By night it was chucking it down again, so I pitched my tent under two baobab trees, also known as upside-down trees, for shelter. The local story goes that when they were first created, these trees were placed near a lake in which they could see their own reflection, and they thought they were ugly, so they complained to their Creator. The Creator was deeply offended so picked them out of their roots, flipped them upside down and plonked them back into the dirt. So it now looks like their roots grow on top.

Collecting water was one of our biggest challenges on this leg. There was barely any around, so we piled as much as possible into our rucksacks, in spite of the weight. Over the course of that first week, my body got used to the weight of the rucksack, and Mi and I worked well together. After a long day's trekking, we'd just walk to the top of a sand dune and find a tiny patch in which both our tents could fit.

This was the land of Antandroy, which in Malagasy means "the spiny people" or "people of the thorn bush" – named for the short, spiky shrubs and big cactus. It was a dry land, and an extremely tough life. Hopefully the rainy season offered them more, but with the rainy seasons came big cyclones, which killed hundreds of people each year there. What lay ahead was more greenery, more forest, more wetland and on towards my goal, the mountains.

We were maybe one or two days away from Fort-Dauphin when we joined a small road, and came across more villages, everyone living in huts fenced around by cactus. We were walking down a hill towards a dry river bed when we saw three young people walking towards us in the distance; it looked as though they were carrying baskets of laundry. All of a sudden they saw us, dropped everything and sprinted away down the sandy bank. We were shocked, but later learned there were bandits around, and cattle had gone missing. Some bandits were known to take children. Maybe they thought we were bandits and they were running for their lives. At the next village, the people ran away too.

Arriving at a village, aching, hurting, tired, we usually just wanted a bit of hospitality, maybe someone to help us get water and food so we could move on. Unfortunately, in the next place we stopped there was a drunken guy calling himself the sheriff, demanding to see passports, asking for money, asking for vodka. Everyone surrounded us so tightly there was barely any room to get into my rucksack, trying to sell us stuff, putting their hands out and asking for money. Meanwhile, the elders told us some people were scared that white people would kidnap them and take their organs. We got the water we needed, and got out as fast as we could.

Mostly the people we met were genuinely friendly and hospitable, but they were often quite desperate, and sometimes wanted to charge me money to stay on their land. It was sad to be seen as an ATM, but obviously I had more money than they did.

On the other side of a dry river bed, we met a local guy who started speaking to Mi in Malagasy. He was skinny, gangly, wearing an over-large white Adidas jacket with a granddad hat, a flat cap. He didn't speak any English, but Mi said he offered to let us camp on his land, a few kilometres away, with just a few huts and no children, so there'd be no babies crying or cockerels crowing at 4am – something I'd started to be wary of. We agreed, and started walking with him. I couldn't shake the feeling that he looked a bit dodgy, though I couldn't put my finger on why – something about his face reminded me of The Joker in the Batman films. Mi stopped to pull a thorn out of his foot, and as I walked on, the guy came up to me, gave me a sideways look that freaked me out, and covering his mouth, whispered, *in English*, "Give me your money."

I ignored him, but now didn't trust him in the slightest. We reached his huts and they weren't what he'd promised at all. So we left and continued to walk yet again. Thankfully a little further on we met another guy who said we could sleep on his land free of charge. There was an abandoned house on a beautiful lake below some plantation fields, and we could relax in peace.

As we left the desert behind, the landscape changed abruptly: we crossed a hill and suddenly it was all green and lush, with more forest on the hills. We saw more wildlife – I spotted a lemur, a snake, and a chameleon. We were now with the people of the forest, who spoke a different dialect again – there are 18 different dialects relating to the different landscapes. Mi had been struggling with the "spiny" dialect, but understood the forest people a lot better. The water sources were still basic, however. We came across a muddy puddle that cars and bikes were driving through, and cattle were drinking from, and were shocked to see people drawing water with jugs and buckets to drink from it. That was how desperate people got in the dry season. A guy offered us some water from a bottle; we accepted and I tried to filter it but it still seemed to taste of dirt.

At a big village not far from Fort-Dauphin, we treated ourselves to zebu and rice and Coca Cola; then an hour or two later, we went back to the same place and had chicken with rice and a cup of tea, and found a little hut to stay in for about £3. It saved putting the tent up so we could leave early next morning, just get out of bed and start walking. It was a huge 21-mile day of walking but on a straightforward road.

We woke at 5am and set out while it was still cool. The sun was slowly coming over the mountain in the distance and it would heat up, but it was just a question of powering forward, walking and walking and walking, and getting the distance done. We stopped for breakfast, a kind of doughnuts, little rolls of bread coated in a layer of sugar, and tea which was just hot water and sugar – pretty unhealthy but it gave us the energy to keep going.

The day's walk was beautiful – between valleys, mountains and paddy fields, and the colours were so vibrant – the green was a vivid green, the blue sky dazzling. Seeing people working in the paddy fields reminded me of Vietnam. I thought about the last eight days; it felt good, exploring at its rawest, with no camera crew, no support crew. Just Mi, a local Malagasy. Being out in the wild, with nothing… That was what I was here for.

The last couple of miles were a killer. We stopped to sort our blisters out, and each step was a painful step; but finally, we made it to Fort-Dauphin. I found a cheap hotel room, planning to rest for three days. It was strange, after over a week of desert and ocean, to be around traffic noise and lots of people again. I had meetings with conservationists and with my second guide, and I sent stuff I didn't need to Antananarivo.

# 8: Fort-Dauphin to Tsarasoa: crocodiles, plague and a man with a gun

There had been more shooting between the bandits and the military, and soldiers had been killed and injured. The bandits were hiding in the bush, the military were looking for the bandits, and we didn't want to get in between. On his way to Fort-Dauphin, Joe had heard of two drivers being shot and killed. So this next area was going to be extremely dangerous. I'd have to avoid any paths and hack my way through the jungle to stay hidden.

Joe was waiting for me as I arranged, but Mi now said he'd do anything to join us on the next 30-day leg. After the drinking incident on the first day of the expedition, he'd been good and we got on well during the tough eight-day trek. I liked the enthusiasm but made it clear I could only pay for one guide, so they said they'd split the food and water costs. There was at first a bit of rivalry and showing off between them, but I told them they were being unprofessional and they put a stop to it. Now there would be three of us, and it would be good to face the challenges together.

While in the city I had a meeting with a conservation group who were working to protect the forest and the wildlife living in it, and to educate young people. Though certain species were becoming extinct, they were discovering new species on a weekly basis; and they were planting and protecting trees that were endemic to Madagascar. Six years earlier, there was a part of the rainforest on the coast where the lemurs were being hunted for food. It had been a long process since then to build up the lemurs' trust in order for them to be comfortable around humans, and it was humbling and inspiring to know there were people like that endeavouring to protect the wildlife.

As I set off with Joe and Mi, we were already starting to see more mountains, and it was greener, with an abundance of fruit and vegetables – oranges, mangoes. We also saw a fair few spiders and snakes. We came across our first river, but still being on the main road, it was easy – there was a barge, mainly used for the carts pulled by zebu, the cattle with their angular bones and upturned horns. It was nice not to have to swim just yet. The temperature was still about 35–40°Celsius, and it would be a lot hotter in the humid jungle and the mountains. It was certainly an incredibly diverse and beautiful island.

The life didn't seem so difficult in this area, though people were still living in huts without electricity. We came across some locals who kept pointing at my bag and trying to pick it up, saying that even the military don't carry that much weight. I'd weighed my bag after sending 7kg back, and it was now 25kg (so I was probably carrying 32kg for the first eight days). Mi was carrying close to 20kg, and Joe 16kg. But obviously I'd trained hard and Joe and Mi both seemed to be suffering already, limping with some major blisters on the go. Was I walking too fast? I had a bit of a crack in my foot, but was feeling on form and blocking out the pain. It generally takes two weeks to rub the dust off and break into my wild side.

It was worrying me that the bandits were close. We'd seen a village that had been completely burned down; it was a sad sight. At Manantenina, we stopped to rest for a day as Joe's foot was in a lot of pain. I had electronics to charge anyway, as we'd be in the bush for the next couple of weeks. There we met a man who'd been working at a mine when the miners had fled because the bandits were getting closer. There were reported to be a hundred, two hundred bandits and they were shooting anyone they encountered. We looked at the maps with this man, and it turned out that my idea to hide in the jungle wouldn't work because the bandits were using the jungle to hide from the military. If we didn't want to get caught in the crossfire, we'd have to continue along the coast for a while. And they were coming fast so we needed to get moving.

Mi started drinking again that night – fretting a little, worried about the next section, as all three of us were. We'd settle down, happy with the route, sure we'd be OK if we stayed aware, then Mi got Joe and me panicked by saying all sorts of random, crazy stuff, that the thieves would shoot him and Joe and take me hostage to get money from the government. Whether or not he'd heard rumours, the fear in both their faces was real. And it made me worried too, thinking that this wasn't a place ruled by law and order; it was completely corrupt and these guys were armed with guns. But we had a good plan of action now; we'd move up the coast and head for the mountains once we'd passed the danger zone.

Soon there were more rivers to cross, some a couple of hundred metres wide. One time we had to jump in a dugout canoe steered by a local; we crouched on tiptoes with our backpacks on for the 300-metre crossing, which was quite painful. The weather turned rainy and windy, and we got slightly lost, crossing so many little streams and areas of boggy, muddy marshland that eventually I just walked across in my trainers, sometimes up to my knees in the water, in the rain and wind. Who cared? It was an adventure! In the evening, camping in the bush after the rain stopped, I tried to dry out my stuff.

My tent seemed to struggle in this environment, leaking in more and more water as the days went by – perhaps there were a couple of small rips in the material – and a lot of things were wet, including my sleeping bag. It was a high quality, super-lightweight tent, but it wasn't holding up well in these extremes. I needed my Mongolia tent, which had withstood all sorts of crazy weather. Making a fire took a while but we made noodles and turned in early, falling asleep to the sound of cicadas and the light of a bright full moon. We woke up to find that a rat had been feasting on our rations, opening up the packets of noodles and even the coffee sachets.

We crossed into Fianarantsoa region. The landscape looked to me at times like a mix between the African plains and the Mongolian steppe: undulating lands of warm, ochre grassland, set off by the deep green of the trees, with more plantations and vegetation as we headed north. We came across a tree like bamboo called ravenala, whose branches flared out like a fan, with glossy palm-type leaves at the end. Joe taught me that if you cut the branches in the middle they provide you with clean drinking water; for this reason they're known as the traveller's palm. Pollinated by lemurs, they are native to Madagascar. One day I spotted a chameleon and chased it with my camera; it changed colour from green to black – the colour of my T-shirt.

Mi and Joe and I were working well as a team, averaging 13–14 miles a day, and ticking the days off until we could hit the mountains. At a village where we stopped for food, we asked the sheriff if it was safe to head inland to the bush. He said the bandits were now in Befasy, only around 20km away. So we'd have to stick to the coast for a little longer.

On day 21, we were invited to stay in a hut, quite a large hut made of wooden planks, with a few rooms inside, and several other buildings crowded close together on the dirt track that passed through the settlement. It was very kind of the local people, but during the night I was attacked by mosquitoes and there were rats all over the room – above me, below me, making a racket. We got only a few hours' sleep, and I woke up to rat droppings on my bed and red marks on my body. I preferred the tent – it provided a layer of protection.

Usually I got a better night's sleep camping outside of the community; it was easier just to pitch somewhere with a nice cool breeze. But Joe and Mi always wanted to sleep near other people, regardless of rats and mosquitoes and cockroaches running everywhere. Maybe they had some fears of the bush. When we reached a bigger place like Vangaindrano, which was poor but had electricity, at least I could do some recharging and washing. Soon we would head inland.

***

I was fascinated by my brushes with the Malagasy culture. Once while walking this section, I saw men in a field who seemed to be wrestling with zebu. I went over to investigate and learned it was a tradition: they chased the zebu around a flooded rice paddy to plough up the ground for planting seeds, sometimes wrestling the cattle into the mud for fun. Another time, we stumbled upon some sort of festival in a village, with dancing. I was keen to watch, but instead, when people caught sight of me, they all came running over and surrounded me in a mad frenzy.

At one village, we got into a debate about crocodiles. The Malagasy believed that the crocodiles had a deal with locals and wouldn't attack them while they swam across a river. I was pretty sure that if you met a crocodile while out swimming, it wouldn't stop and ask where you were from. Then there was the belief about leaves and snakes. If a leaf fell from above, they believed there was a snake hiding in the tree, warning you, and if you stuck around and a second leaf fell, the snake would spear itself through your skull. I would always wind the lads up for a laugh if there was a little rustle or a leaf dropped – I'd shout out and watch them panic.

The local people also believed in setting fire to fields – sometimes to allow new grass to grow, but also because the smoke would turn to clouds and that would bring rain. They'd do it when there hadn't been rain for a while, and of course sometimes it would rain afterwards reinforcing the belief, so for generations the uneducated people in remote places believed that was how rain was created.

Although I always want to learn from the locals when I travel, and have learned so much, you have to have a filter too, as they aren't always right. Many locals told me it was impossible to walk from here up to the far north of Madagascar; that it couldn't be done. It made me chuckle because it was the same in Mongolia. Most people had no idea of distances either, because they were unaccustomed to walking far; I knew that much just from asking directions. From the first trip when Mat and I were told it wasn't possible to cross the border from Cambodia to Vietnam and then cycle the length of Vietnam on £10 bikes, I knew to take what people said with a pinch of salt – especially when they said something couldn't be done.

Joe and Mi were finding the trek difficult. As I packed up one morning, with villagers peering over the long grass at me, Joe and Mi talked about money, about their families, saying they were never given the easy expedition. After all he'd said to convince me to bring him along, Mi was now regretting joining us on this leg. It was disappointing – but a reminder of just how tough the expedition was at times. I was mentally stronger as I was prepared for months of this, whereas they only had weeks, a much smaller goal. If I went solo, I'd be able to focus without any negativity rubbing off on me; I seem to power on regardless of the conditions when I'm alone. But they were good lads and perhaps it was just a matter of not fully understanding each other's ways due to the language barrier. Later on, we stopped for lunch at a common village and as we headed off again in heat that approached 40°C, I chatted with Joe about life and work. It made a difference, smoothed things over.

People often assume that if you come from the West, you're loaded. Since my Mongolia expedition, I'd given a lot of talks to groups, especially young people in schools and colleges, about how my adventures began, from coming up with a plan at the age of 16, getting qualifications that would enable me to work abroad, selling my car and so on. My adventures and achievements had all been on a shoestring budget and people were often surprised. They could relate to me more when they found out I came from an ordinary background, with a normal education, with no wealth or special privileges.

Joe had had a tough beginning in life: he was abandoned as a toddler by his mum, and had to rely on begging and the goodness of the local people. He grew up on the streets where he met other street kids and learned how to stay alive from them. There was fighting and stealing. He was spotted by a couple from Réunion who had recently opened a shelter for street kids, helping to teach them skills so they could get jobs and go on to live a normal life. His story of rising above that start to where he was today was pretty inspirational, and he took great pride in telling it, happy now to have a job and a family.

We stopped walking early when we reached a small village, finding a place to camp on an unused paddy field. We listened to music, with a mass of young children breakdancing around us. It was a great atmosphere. Then the kids, aged about six or seven, asked something I thought perhaps I misunderstood, so I asked Joe and Mi.

"Yes, they are asking if we want women to have sex with tonight."

I was shocked – and in stitches with laughter.

We woke up to loud reggae music, which was surprisingly nice, and 35-degree heat which was a bit worrying at 7am. I went to get pancakes and tea with Mi, then we headed off down a beautiful track, watching people busy doing their work, in the paddy fields or collecting wood, all happy, smiling and saying hello – and sometimes laughing at me.

In the afternoon, we were walking through forest on a narrow path when we came to a river. Gilles had said that every river in Madagascar has crocodiles, but that they didn't properly wake up – hungry and aggressive after hibernating – until November, December. It was only October and the river seemed to come to a dead end, so Joe and Mi said they doubted there would be any. We decided to jump in, but I noticed the lads were hesitant to go in the muddy, deep section. I went in slightly deeper to wash, but after I had sat in the water for five minutes a local came over, shouting in Malagasy. The expression of panic said it all, and we leapt out. He said there were crocodiles here up to four metres long. Yikes!

We walked over hills with long grass and paddy fields, seeing small lakes in the distance. The temperature reached into the 40s, but we took a break every hour in the shade. The terrain made the walk interesting: swamp land, rivers, steep hills and broken bridges. A local warned us of bandits ahead who had stolen zebu from his village the night before. That particular danger wasn't over yet.

On 6th October, the day that marked the end of the first month of the expedition, we had a breakfast of the doughnuts they call mofo with sugar tea, and started a big climb: we were finally working our way up to mountains, which was the main event of the expedition. It was beautiful and quiet – just the noises of nature. When, around noon, we came across a river with rapids, it was a no-brainer: the lads and I got straight in, screaming and laughing at how cold and refreshing the water was. Then we washed our clothes too, chilled out for a couple of hours. A couple of local girls on the opposite bank were also washing clothes, and there was not a cloud in the sky.

We hit the track again, passing a few cyclists who were taking a rest, and saying hello to them. Soon after, we too decided to take a break in the shade of the trees at the side of the road to drink some water, noticing how dry the vegetation was after a run of hot days. We saw the same young guys cycle past us, pretty fast – they didn't stop to say hello this time. We thought nothing of it. Just ten minutes later, we heard crackling noises but had no idea what it was. It sounded like bike gears being changed, so I assumed more cyclists were coming. I was just looking down at some photos on my phone and I noticed ash falling on the screen – but again I took no notice, thinking it was something from the trees.

Then Joe stood up and looked to where we'd just come from, and started sniffing the air. I stood up and so did Mi. We could see more ash falling. The crackling noise got louder. A warm breeze was blowing our way.

Joe said, "Quick – we need to leave *now*. That's a forest fire!"

We had no idea how big it was, but it was getting close fairly fast.

We scrambled up, threw the rucksacks on and walked as fast as we could along the path under the overhanging trees. Thankfully we made it out of the forest and the land opened up to hills ahead, bare except for rocks or dead grass. We seemed to leave the fire behind, but it was quite an adrenaline rush.

We kept walking longer than usual in order to replenish the water supplies as the lads had run out. At a tiny village in a valley with mountains on either side, the people weren't particularly talkative but we knew it was a sign of disrespect to arrive in a village after dark, as we had; without electricity, it was hard for them to see you properly. There were 30 or 40 people, no more than a dozen huts made of clay or dung, and they said we could camp and use their stove to cook; but kept their distance and told us to sleep outside in the tent. Then the sheriff told Joe the reason why: the rats in the village had fleas, and the fleas carried disease. Gilles had warned me a while ago that some of the small communities still suffered from bubonic plague.

I now felt quite freaked out and paranoid, and knew I had to stay covered and away from rats, cats and dogs. We could see the glow of the fire in the distance on the hills, lighting up the sky above it, the smoke rising. The locals gave us an eel to eat, and we ate quickly in the light of our head-torches, wanting to get inside the tent away from the scavenging dogs, and the mosquitoes that were flying around our heads; we could switch the head-torches off but then we wouldn't see if flies landed on the food. I was so tired that, in spite all this, I managed to sleep.

The next morning, I woke up to cockerels and babies crying and dogs barking, and went to retrieve my backpack. All the locals were standing around, and Joe and Mi said good morning to them but they didn't reply. I wondered if they'd recently lost a relative to plague, or the bandits had got to their cattle. It seemed an eerie atmosphere. We made some tea just from boiled water with a spoonful or two of sugar – and it seemed all three of us were suffering with diarrhoea, which must have been from dodgy eel the night before – but we laughed about it. It was a nice morning and as far as we could see, the fire in the distance had died down. I got ready, drank some water, put sun cream on my nose, went to pick up my bag and throw it over my shoulder, keen to get going – and there was a rat.

Of all the villages where I had to get a rat under my bag, it had to be the one that might have bubonic plague. For a moment I just stared. Then the rat ran out and the locals went crazy, panicking, even the kids and the ladies, all ages, all sizes, chased this rat around the mud patch, trying to stamp on it – it ran past Joe, who lifted his leg up and gave a little scream before joining the chase – but the rat was dodging everyone. It leaped up onto an old tyre and went inside, but a dog followed it, caught it and ate it. All in all, I was happy to get moving. We decided against brushing our teeth or loading up on water from that village.

The smooth, low hills were covered in dry-looking grassland and once we stopped at a well with a pump on the edge of a paddy field to cool off. We stopped for lunch at Maropaika, eating pork and rice in what looked like someone's empty bedroom with just a table and bed inside. Joe and Mi said they'd never walked in such hot temperatures and I could see they were struggling. I'd felt this heat many times before and adapted fast to it, but I knew it could drain their energy and be dangerous – I remembered the Gobi Desert – so I was thankful to be in good health and spirits. We topped up with water regularly and took breaks at least every hour when we found a tree to provide some shade. Another time we were walking when we met a girl carrying sugar cane sticks. We asked her if she could spare one, and smiling away, she gave us one to share. It was so tasty with lots of energy packed into it – perfect for walking.

A few days later, we were walking between a couple of villages when a guy in military uniform, with a gun over his shoulder, demanded to see my passport. He had a civilian friend with him and they were both drunk. I dug in my bag and, advised by Mi, handed over instead the papers signed by the tourism minister that I'd been carrying since the outset. These said how many days we should be in which section of the island and what I was doing.

"No good," he said. According to the dates on the paper, we should have been out of the south section and in Fianarantsoa by 30 September. It was now 7 October. This came as a surprise, but through some typo or whatever, the tourism office had got the date wrong, and no-one had pointed this out before. The drunken military officer instantly seized that and started to get aggressive with me, swinging his gun. Maybe he thought I was French – the Malagasy have a slight thing against the French due to past troubles – and was picking any excuse to have a go at me. Or maybe he just wanted money. Or maybe he was genuinely serious and angry that I was travelling with invalid paperwork.

I got my passport out and showed him that I had a six-month visa stamped in it, allowing me to remain in Madagascar until March – I was only a month into it. Unfortunately, he only became more aggressive, creating a commotion. Locals started to gather round. I sensed that they were on my side but fearful of saying anything to the military. The soldier demanded that I pay him 100,000 ariary, around £20. When I laughed and refused, he said we had to walk six miles back to Maropaika. Again I refused, which further upset him.

He started shouting at Joe and Mi, and both guides looked worried at this point. They tried to explain, but he was clearly telling them to shut up and not speak back to him. I could tell from Joe's face that he was thinking of doing something. We knew the officer was in the wrong but what could we do? The officer had either an M16 over his shoulder, pointing our way. It slipped off his shoulder a few times as he was shouting and he was catching it by the handle, pretty much by the trigger. I dodged out of the way, looking to see if the safety catch was on. Would we have to grab the weapon off him – was that possible – knowing he was in the wrong and we'd be defending ourselves against a drunk guy with a gun? We needed to get out of this situation and we needed to act fast.

It went on for close to half an hour, with the military officer demanding higher and higher amounts of money and me refusing. I was lucky to have Joe and Mi with me to explain what he was saying. Things weren't calming down at all. His drunken civilian pal had come at me like he wanted to fight me; the crowd had been holding him back, but he lashed out until they let him go and came right towards me. I dropped my bag.

*"Bonjour vaz'ha,"* the guy said in a confrontational way; it meant "Hello foreigner" and was mainly addressed to white people.

I couldn't run – there was an officer with a gun – so I'd have to stay and if he started swinging I'd have to fight. Being a trained Muay Thai fighter and in good shape, I was confident about my fighting abilities but didn't want it to come to that, even if I was only defending myself.

I replied, *"Salam' Malagas."*

I had my hand up pretending to scratch my chin, ready to guard or block a punch if it came. We continued staring each other down with evil looks. *If I turn around, he'll swing,* I thought. I stood my ground, face to face with him. Then another man, stepping forward, grabbed the man by the arm and dragged him away. That just left the drunken soldier with the gun, with whom I argued for another 25 minutes or so until two more military guys arrived, one of them a captain. This was either going to make matters worse, I thought, or they'd be on our side.

Joe and Mi explained our story, and the two sober military men listened calmly. The drunken soldier was still shouting abuse, but the sober officers pretty much told him to hush and move on. They apologised to the three of us, and allowed us to go. As we were leaving, they asked for money – but it was only the equivalent of 20 pence, so I thought, *let's just give it to them*; it would get them a cup of tea.

Before we walked off, they added that they were searching for bandits known to be in the area, and suggested for the sake of our security that we camp in the nearby village. It was getting late so we had little choice. Thankfully the villagers were welcoming. They crowded around us as we entered the village, everyone looking excited, some running away to fetch friends and family while others ran towards us to greet us. Everyone was full of smiles and there were three times as many kids as adults – it was loud with shouting and laughter. The sheriff of the village came over with a huge smile, shaking our hands and welcoming us to his community, which seemed a fairly well-kept place of scattered mud and wooden huts, at the top of a small hill which offered a cool breeze. The sun was setting and it bathed the place in golden light, as the sheriff offered us different places to sleep.

Word had got around about what had happened, and everyone agreed that the drunken officer had been in the wrong. It was the village's anniversary and there was a festival, and apparently the officer had been drunk all day, and the civilians couldn't wait for him to go. Masses of excited children surrounded me and the only way I could escape was to go inside a concrete hut and close the door, so they opened up the windows. The hut was crawling with spiders, but I was just happy that the situation had calmed down and I was in a better place, with some good people.

# 9: Tsarasoa to Fianarantsoa: malaria, a big mountain, and a hangover

The next night, we stayed at a big district village and I saw Mi crying on the phone. Joe explained that Mi was telling his mum about his sore, blistered feet; his mum started crying and that upset him too. I felt bad, so the lads told me something to make me laugh. It turned out that around the dinner table the previous night, the girls had been harassing them, saying they liked me and wanted to try having sex with a *vazaha*. The lads had stood outside the door to keep the girls out, and I'd slept through the whole thing unaware.

Determined to make it to Tsarasoa soon, we had some long, hot days of walking on tracks across wide open savannahs, with the occasional river to scramble across or a patch of forest. We covered as much distance as possible and I loved it. We'd try to camp near a water source to cook food, collect water wherever we could. On one of the toughest days so far, we walked for 12 hours, then the ground was so hard we couldn't get the tent pegs in, so we found a tiny sloping patch of mud surrounded by rocks, and squeezed both tents onto it. Just a sugar tea for breakfast at dawn, and then we were off again, crossing paddy fields, swamp land, mountains, boulders – really varied terrain. We finally made it to the town and treated ourselves to a big meal and a cold Coke, followed by a celebratory beer.

Tsarasoa was one of the most beautiful places I've ever seen, with massive towers of grey rock rising out of the gentle, lush valley, and 15 or 16 different communities; remote, but less so than where I'd come from, it was the location of the eco-lodge belonging to my logistics manager Gilles, with small bungalows scattered on the side of a hill, each with a solar panel on top for light; and there were one or two restaurants serving Western food. I'd been here six months before on the recce. I was a month into my expedition, only about 20 percent through, but it was good to be back here. I'd visualised arriving here in my plans, and I'd made it. We checked into a hotel where Mi's mum worked. Joe would be leaving soon, and Mi would continue with me, heading to Pic Boby, the second highest mountain in Madagascar, the first of the eight I planned to summit.

In the town, I met some European travellers here to do adventure trips, some cycling 100km or rock climbing or driving around the island in small groups. They were taken aback to hear what I was doing.

I started to get a bit of a headache, but assumed it was because I'd been pushing so hard and was finally at a place where I could relax. I let my body recover from the blisters and the painful rubbing of my rucksack, but I felt quite dehydrated. The next day I was feeling even worse, but I'd booked to go paragliding – my first time ever.

A paragliding instructor lived in a nearby village, and he came to take me up to one of the sheer clifftops, a good hour or two's trek to the top. It was stupidly hot in the valley, and I could see fields burning not so far away. Despite my headache, I scrambled up the cliff face. It was difficult – I took my top off and was dripping with sweat. Joe was the same – he came up with me because the instructor couldn't speak much English and I needed a translator. It made me a bit nervous, about to jump off a cliff when I wasn't sure I fully understood the instructions. All I was told was to run off the cliff – just keep running until I was off the ground, then get into sitting position…

I strapped myself in. We did a three-second countdown and then, "Run run run!"

We were running fast towards the edge of the cliff. A few metres in the air, I got myself in the sitting position, but this was a bad thing.

"No, run run run!!"

So I jumped back out of the seat and continued running towards the ledge, and he shouted: "Stop stop stop!!!"

A couple of metres from the edge, running towards it, we had to stop the paraglider.

Luckily we managed to stop, and the paraglider dropped in front of us. We went back and he explained a little bit better the second time around. Now I felt nerves kick in – I had to make sure I got this right.

We started again: "Run run run!" And quickly we got some good air and flew off the cliff. It was incredible to be looking down into the beautiful valley on a hot, sunny day with no clouds, out over the land I'd walked across and the land ahead.

We flew for around eight minutes, relying not on heat thermals but the wind – which wasn't constant, and every time the wind dropped, we did too. No-one had told me about the landing. We were dropping quite fast, and I heard the instructor panic, saying, "Oh oh oh!" And then, "So sorry Ash…" I began to worry what was up. Then he told me to stand and the parachute hit a tree, and we landed on a paddy field. The locals working on it looked around, confused.

It had been a great experience. But that evening whilst relaxing in my circular one-roomed bungalow, big enough to fit in a bed and a shelf for belongings, I was definitely feeling worse, with diarrhoea and a banging headache. I went to bed early, and when I woke the next morning I was in a bit of pain and couldn't make it to breakfast. I later got some food down me, figuring it was heat exhaustion as I'd had similar symptoms, though much worse, in the Gobi Desert – headache, eyes hurting, a little bit delirious. I told myself to drink lots of water, get lots of sugar and salt, and I decided to postpone our departure until I was feeling 100 percent again. The people looked after me, giving me medicinal tea and hand massages. I sniffed some extremely strong scent that seemed good for my head and they moved me to a bigger room to keep me cool. I took some paracetamol and ibuprofen and had a pretty restless, sweaty night's sleep, but felt slightly better the next morning.

Mi came to check on me, and brought me some breakfast, saying he'd go to ask the doctor to come and see me. I was pretty sure it was dehydration but thought it best to check. He also heard there were two French doctors in a nearby village with a local Malagasy guide and he went to see them. They came by to check on me while hiking past, which was very kind of them. I'd begun to worry that I might have contracted malaria, but they told me it couldn't be malaria as I seemed too upbeat – I wouldn't be smiling, I wouldn't even be standing if I had malaria – so it must be heat exhaustion. I was relieved. They said to drink Coke, water, and get lots of sugar and salt and rice down me, and I'd recover in no time. So I added lots of salt to my chicken and chips, had lots of Coke, water and pineapple juice, with a paracetamol and two ibuprofen, and started feeling pretty damn good already, full of energy and ready for action.

Yet again, though, I had a bad night's sleep, and the next day I was worse.

All sorts of thoughts go through your mind when you're in pain, especially when it's inside you. I'd heard stories of people dying fast due to heat exhaustion; although I had recovered in the Gobi, there was an irrational worry in the back of my mind that maybe this time it would finish me off. Whenever I had thoughts like that, I'd get up and drink water to try to regain my positivity, which was hard when I didn't have energy to do anything. I knew I needed one good night's sleep, which would make me a whole lot better. I couldn't eat, forced liquids into me, and had a crazy amount of wind. I was told to have a massage, which turned out to be soothing; I went for a shower then straight to bed with a soaked bandanna to keep me cool.

I woke up feeling slightly refreshed, but still couldn't drink or eat much. Although I was struggling, I hoped I was on the road to recovery. Mi and his mum kept checking on me. I received an email saying they had found me a suitable guide; Capital FM and an Italian journalist wanted to interview me; but I didn't feel capable of doing interviews or speaking to a potential new guide. I tried to stay in my room, hidden in the shade, but the bungalow had two big windows and I had to keep the door open for air, so it was impossible to escape from the sun. If I didn't sleep well and felt worse in the morning, I'd arrange to be taken to Fianarantsoa, the second biggest city in Madagascar, to get a cool room and be looked at by another doctor.

The night wasn't good at all. It was the fourth or fifth night like this and I was hallucinating, constantly woken by nightmares. I remember being half-asleep, delirious, semi-conscious. I was desperate for water, and there was a glass of water right next to me on the table. It was hard to sit up, as I was in a lot of pain, and there were two voices in my head: one good, saying you need to drink, sit up now and DRINK – while the other was bad, saying don't worry about that, go to sleep, it will be a painless death, over before you know. It was terrifying yet soothing at the same time. This debate lasted for close to an hour before I forced myself to sit up and drink. At that point, I knew I had to get out of there.

I got up, wrapped a towel around me in slow motion, really struggling to get to the reception area. Mi's mum was working and I told her I needed to get to the hospital in Fianarantsoa. She felt my head and could tell from my temperature that that was what I needed to do. She organised a vehicle. Feeling absolutely horrendous, I prepared for the three-hour journey, just grabbing the essentials. Mi came with me.

I sat in the front passenger seat of the 4x4 where I'd have access to a window. The first hour or so was on bumpy dirt tracks, which was painful for my body, and the sun was beaming straight down on me, which only made it worse. But we finally arrived and Mi found me a room at the best hotel in the city, the kind of place with hundreds of rooms and a restaurant. I noticed in a dazed way that my room was cool with a fan, before collapsing on the bed and falling asleep. I woke up now and again and saw Mi sitting nearby, but it was all blurry and in slow motion. Sporadically he ordered me things like yoghurt and water and banana milkshake, though I didn't even end up touching them as I had no energy to feed myself.

I saw two faces looking down at me on the bed. I was still hallucinating, and their faces and voices were blurry, but they sat me up, which woke me, and I realised they were the doctors. One of the doctors spoke to me in broken English. She took my temperature and blood pressure, which were both extremely bad. She then took a blood test and very quickly, she looked at me with concern and told me that I had contracted the deadliest strain of malaria, *falciparum*.

My heart truly sank. I was devastated. I thought: malaria is the biggest killer in human history, and once you have malaria, you have it for life. That was it, I thought. The deadliest strain usually kills you within 24 hours, but I had hung on for five days. Maybe my anti-malaria pills were still trying to work, but the diarrhoea I had from the eel meant I wasn't keeping the medication in my system; the small amount of it my body retained had allowed me to hang on those vital extra days. The doctor gave me pills immediately. I vomited and still had bad diarrhoea. That night I sweated and shivered, sweated and shivered.

Sleep is so incredibly important. I woke up feeling much better, more able to focus. The doctor came again and started to explain a bit better to me that she could completely eradicate the disease from my body, wipe it completely out of my system, because I'd caught it just at the right time. A few hours later, she said, I could have slipped into a coma. But if I did exactly what she said, took the medication she prescribed, drank lots and ate well, then I could make a full recovery. I started taking the drugs and of course did everything she said.

It was scary knowing I was only a quarter of the way through Madagascar and had had such a ridiculous amount thrown at me already. Every day had been a struggle, it seemed, and I worried that I might catch malaria again. I just wanted to complete the rest of the expedition with only the challenges of the mountains, the walking – no more diseases or water/food poisoning. Having gone through this was giving me negative feelings about Madagascar – the people, the climate – and I wanted to just get the expedition done and go home. But I knew it was just the pills and illness talking. And sure enough, the next day I got my positivity back.

I tried to listen to what my body wanted to eat, as the doctor advised; it was asking for pizza, so I ordered room service. I struggled to eat – after a few mouthfuls I had to run for the bathroom – but when the doctor came round again, already my temperature and blood pressure had come down a good amount. I took the tablets, spoke to my parents and little brother, and slept.

For the next seven days I was restricted to the hotel room, which was by far the most luxurious I'd stayed in. They couldn't let me go to the hospital because the malaria was infectious, and if a mosquito bit me and then someone else, it would spread. But the doctor visited twice a day. My appetite slowly started to return. I was very skinny, all the fat stripped off my body, but mentally I was sharp again. I spoke to my mum again, and having done research she was deeply worried.

"It's not a cold," she said, "it's malaria. You need to come back home and fully recover." She said the insurance company had a helicopter on stand-by, and she and my dad thought I should be evacuated out.

But that wasn't an option. I didn't see it as a time to quit.

*Damn you to hell, Madagascar!* I wasn't having it. I wouldn't let it beat me. I visualised Madagascar as an enemy, and the anger provided me with energy. This was the perfect time to rise to the challenge. It was time to quit and go home, or rise up and shine. Fight or flight. I had to face it. I had to make a full recovery and crack on. I was lucky to be in safe hands. There were phone calls between my insurance company and the doctor seeing me and she was doing everything spot-on. She acted at the perfect time and was providing me with the right medication. I knew I was in safe hands and this was my chance to fully recover. The whole thing had given me a huge scare, but I would continue with the expedition.

I started planning the route out, organising how I should go about it, how I'd protect myself from malaria and exhaustion, looking in the mirror and telling myself to look after myself, stay focused, alert, determined and above all, finish what I started. Madagascar wasn't going to stop me that easily. I started to get restless and bored, ready to crack on.

On the last day, I went in the indoor swimming pool at the hotel, and saw that as a positive step towards getting my strength back. Training has always been an important way of re-energising, for me. Walking around the city, facing the sun, I was feeling better. I asked the doctor if I could push on, and she said as long as I finished my medication – because I still had malaria, she reminded me – as long as I kept taking it whilst I was walking, it would kill the malaria. I did some push-ups and pull-ups in my room, preparing myself mentally for heading back into the unknown. I wondered what would happen on the remaining three-quarters of the journey. I started to feel excited about the expedition again, and went through everything, making sure I had enough money for the national park, guide, food and so on.

The next morning I ordered an empty bowl with a spoon for my Coco Pops – always difficult to translate, that one – and Mi knocked on the door saying the driver wanted to leave because he thought it would rain. I could tell Mi was still slightly drunk from the night before; he said he'd started drinking because the police stopped him to check his passport, which he wasn't carrying, then demanded money, and he'd got into a fight with them and been taken back to the station. I couldn't let it bother me. After a week in Fianarantsoa, we left for the three-hour journey back to pick up our kit at Tsarasoa. The next day we would start to climb Pic Boby. Looking back it seems a crazy decision, to climb the second-highest mountain in Madagascar while still on malaria medication, but it seemed right at the time. It helped me regain the strength in my legs, and got me straight back into the swing of things.

My main aim of the expedition was to become the first to walk Madagascar's central ridge, and I had added the peaks to increase the challenge. The highest mountains in Madagascar in order of height are:

Maromokotro – 2876 metres

Pic Boby – 2658 metres

Tsiafajavona – 2643 metres

Andohanisambirano – 2501 metres

Famoizankova – 2367 metres

Inanobe – 2325 metres

Ambohimirahavavy – 2301 metres

Ibity – 2240 metres.

The name Pic Boby came from a group of men who raced to the top and said whoever made it first would have the mountain named after him. They all lost: the dog, Boby, made it to the top ahead of them all. The Malagasy name for Pic Boby is Imarivolanitra, meaning "close to the sky"; Andringitra National Park, where it's situated, is full of granite peaks and waterfalls and the terrain was markedly different from the outset, with bare grey rock pushing through the grassland. Surprisingly, given how barren it looks in places, it's one of the most biologically diverse parts of the island, with many species of plants, birds and frogs living in the forested areas. Mi and I had an obligatory guide with us, who pointed out different plants that were native not only to Madagascar but to that particular national park – they grew there and nowhere else on the planet.

It was tough walking, steep and hot as we scrambled up towards the rest area where we would stop for lunch. Suddenly, as we arrived at the stone-built hut with a straw roof and stone table, we spotted a family of catta lemurs, otherwise known as ring-tailed lemurs because of their black-and-white striped tails. With their thick fur, white faces and black-ringed eyes, it was a treat to see them, presumably taking advantage of the natural spring, looking for food and sunbathing on the roof, as lemurs love to do. These were one of 13 species of lemur found in the park. They jumped up when they saw us approach, and ran off into the distance.

We made rice with green veg for lunch, relaxed and then continued for what was an intense climb. I was surprised how well laid-out the path was, with markers to show the way, as this mountain was fairly well frequented by visitors to the island. The terrain changed swiftly to bare rock and soon it was windy and cool and we were up in the clouds: eerie but beautiful. We saw lemurs again, walking along the boulders and licking moisture from the rocks, which is where they get their minerals and salts from. They live in such harsh conditions – at the top of Pic Boby it's a lunar landscape, there's not much else to survive on.

We eventually made it to base camp, standing at 2,050 metres, over twice the height of our highest mountain in Wales, and it felt great to be there. It was rainy and cold, but it was a relief to feel the chill, although I hoped the cloud would clear by the next day so we'd get a view from the top. I set my tent up quickly under a small shelter; the lads prepared the wood and made sure it was dry as they got the fire ready inside a hut. I added a lot of chilli to my noodles, which the lads found hilarious, then I went off to bed in the hope of a good night's sleep in the cool and the wild emptiness. As I typed up my notes, a big thunderstorm moved in and lightning illuminated the tent, so I could clearly see a rat run right over it.

I left most of my kit in the tent at base camp with Mi for the climb to the peak the next morning. For once, the beast was light on my back! I had sugar tea, biscuits and the remainder of my malaria medication for breakfast, and was really looking forward to the day. As the guide and I set off, it was cool but the clouds had cleared slightly. It took us two and a half hours to scramble to the top, a steep climb up sheer bare rock, but there were stunning views all the way. Finally, with strong winds blowing, we arrived at the peak. It looked like a different planet, the summit a maze of grey-brown rocky outcrops, bare ridges stretching off in all directions, with the clouds now far below us. It felt amazing to have walked to 2,658 metres all the way from sea level, which few people do. It was tough – but it was worth it. I signed the book, took photos and videos, sent out a satellite message and headed back down, grateful to have had such an amazing experience.

At base camp, I packed up to find my tent was broken. The elements had been too extreme and it couldn't cope, ripping inside with the poles bent at an angle. Mi and I continued north, aiming to get to Fianarantsoa in time for my birthday (1st November). It was a stunning walk through immense forest and big mountains; we saw two big waterfalls as we scrambled back down to the 1,000-metre mark. The clouds gathered again and we got battered by the weather. Drenched and cold from the relentless rain, we continued walking. Near the exit from the national park we found some bungalows for rent and decided that due to my tent being broken and neither of our tents being waterproof at the best of times, we'd take a bungalow, dry off, fix my tent as best we could and get some food and a good night's sleep.

Unfortunately, when I got to the kitchen for dinner, I noticed instantly that Mi was wasted. I told him to go to bed, fuming that he'd do this after I'd splashed out on the room and food. The locals took him away to a different room to sleep, and the dinner was enough to put a smile back on anyone's face: soup, rice, chicken and potato, then pineapple and banana in caramel for dessert. Mi knocked on the door at 5:30am. He apologised and said he wouldn't do it again, and that he drank the rum because he was so cold.

We packed and set off on a beautiful, crisp, fresh morning after the storm. The views were stunning, hilly with lots of bright green rice paddy fields. It made for great walking as we were curling around the hills and over them. We were harassed by one drunk old lady who must have followed us for about 3km in an annoying way. Mi, usually so laid-back, got stressed out about this little, frail old lady. I couldn't help laughing when he shooed her off in the end and she miserably stamped her feet as she turned the other way.

Food was always a good incentive to get us to the next destination. When we were hungry – such as when we couldn't find food on a Sunday, with it being church day – we found ourselves talking about what we'd eat when we stopped. The day before we arrived at Fianarantsoa, we were so hungry during a long day's walk that Mi found some old mouldy bread in the bottom of his bag and started eating it. We giggled about that for a while – Mi was good company for his sense of humour, and often one of us would set the other off laughing and we couldn't stop. We set up camp at a beautiful grassy spot with water and a few trees with wood lying around to build a fire, but a thunderstorm moved in fast and rain came pelting down, forcing us into our tents, so we had to eat just dry noodles broken up – like chilli crisps – and that mouldy bread again. We went to sleep hungry, dreaming of all the food we'd order when we got to the next place. We needed good calories and protein in our systems to help our muscles recover overnight, so the morning would be tough. As soon as we found a restaurant for breakfast I ordered five banana fritters, sugar tea, and rice with duck and chilli.

We could see what looked like Fianarantsoa way in the distance, just a vague sense of buildings on the horizon where the forest ended. It was beyond many more hills, loads of ups and downs in the way. It took us a long time to cover the 20 miles, and my bag was killing me. When we eventually made it to the city, I was immensely relieved.

I realised I'd formed a strong bond with Mi, in spite of the drinking incidents, and his English had progressed a lot. Here we were, back in the city where he had stood by me when I had malaria, his mum looking after me. And we'd made good time here through pushing on hard. It was Hallowe'en, and the next day was my birthday. As a celebration, I booked into the same nice hotel – though a different room, after all I'd been through. Mi and I had made a deal that the only time either of us could drink was when we weren't walking the next day, and in Fianarantsoa we were taking a couple of days off. When Mi came to my room, we cracked open a few beers and went downstairs to play pool, snacking on samosas with green chilli sauce – my favourite. I wanted to hit a night club to celebrate a birthday that I hoped I wouldn't forget.

We went out to a bar, a sort of karaoke place in an upstairs room. They gave us the "VIP" section – bare floorboards with one chair and one cushion, curtains drawn around it. We opened the curtains of course, and ordered five samosas each and fries. They misunderstood and brought five big trays, which was way too much, but we didn't care; we got fairly drunk, loud and boisterous, as the place filled up with people partying and dancing to Malagasy music, we made friends with everyone in the bar and invited them to help us eat the food. One thing led to another and we went on to a big club, where I met a lovely, attractive girl who spoke fluent English, among other languages. I joined her and her university friends, talking and drinking. It was a great night – enough said – and the perfect start to my birthday. When I woke up hungover, I realised I probably shouldn't have had so much alcohol while still taking malaria medication… I spent the day trying to get water and healthy food down me, staying in bed and letting my muscles recover for the next section.

# 10: Fianarantsoa to Tana: four peaks, panicked locals and a lot of lemurs

Leaving Fianarantsoa after a great night's sleep, two bowls of Coco Pops and a trip to the ATM, I was glad to be heading back into the bush. Mi and I went over stories from our night out: it had been a long time since I'd drunk alcohol, so it hit me hard. It was a funny night that I'd always remember – just maybe not all the details.

The day was beautiful, a mix of blue skies and fluffy white clouds, and the terrain was easy enough with grassland and trees. We stopped off briefly at Mi's house, a two-roomed brick hut, so I could meet his wife and children; it was a small home for a family of five. Beyond there, we walked beside a wide river, the sun sparkling on the pale grey water as it rippled in the breeze; we needed to cross it but there were crocodiles so we'd have to borrow a dugout canoe from a village of tall huts that Mi knew nearby. Mi paddled us across the river safely.

We were passing the resort where he had worked 10 years before and met his wife, so we stopped to eat at the restaurant.

Mi was excited to catch up with old friends, which was nice to see, so it would have been difficult to say no when they offered us a bungalow at a big discount, just £3 each. But we'd only just left a city, and I didn't particularly want to stay in tourist accommodation when I had a tent. I had to be careful with money, as always, and I was keen to crack on and get back to the bush. Mi would never usually take advantage but he was ordering food and drink that I'd have to pay for – and I could smell alcohol on him, even though we'd made a deal that he wouldn't drink until Tana.

So I felt lonely and ill at ease that evening, staying at the resort, as I thought about this next stretch. We'd be going off-route for a couple of days as I'd agreed to visit the ValBio Centre at Ranomafana National Park, an organisation of the Lemur Conservation Network. After the time I'd lost through illness, it wasn't ideal to take such a lengthy detour, but I'd given my word and wanted to help spread the word about the good work being done. I was feeling mixed emotions, the first time I'd felt that way on the expedition. But once again, I had to take it day by day. One day you'd feel negative – but you can always wait it out until the positive comes back again.

Usually I feel better in the mornings, but that day it wasn't to be. When it came to leaving and paying for the bungalows, they tried to overcharge me. It made me angry: did Mi think I was made of money? We were in a sulk with each other, which made a tough day worse. We were now walking through the rainforest, enclosed by green trees on either side and cloud above, and although the road was easy, it rained and rained. It was awful to know we were in for several long days with clothes and bags drenched – it was unlikely to clear up, being rainforest – and that would lead to difficult evenings. It brought us both down.

We decided to stop at a village as we were both cold and hungry and soaked through, and my blisters were agony. We limped off towards a place Mi knew, hoping to find a spare hut where we could cook. All the locals were hiding inside out of the rain, but the sheriff beckoned us to follow him. I didn't have high expectations, but it turned out he was inviting us to his home and his family welcomed us into a warm, cosy room with two small hard beds and a table. They smiled, seemed happy to have me there and asked questions. They lit candles and boiled water, gave us warm water to wash with, let us dry out our kit. It was a simple but special moment for which I felt very grateful – that warmth and hospitality, just when we needed it.

The next day we made it to the ValBio Centre for conservation near the tourist resort at Ranomafana. The national park was a beautiful place deep in the rainforest, with big brown rivers flowing fast over rapids, waterfalls gushing over cliffs, bamboo thickets and tall trees. Visitors came from all over to conduct research, to watch the birds and the bats, the chameleons and frogs and lemurs. There are over 100 species of lemur, only found in the wild in Madagascar, and they survive by eating fruit, leaving the seeds nicely fertilised to regenerate the forest for the other wildlife.

Lemurs are the world's oldest living primates – lemur-like creatures once roamed Africa with the dinosaurs – and an important link to our evolutionary past, yet they're threatened with extinction. The two main threats are people hunting them for food, and deforestation: Madagascar's forest, the lemurs' habitat, has been severely depleted to make way for farmland. I'd seen fires for myself, some of which might have been started to clear land for growing rice. People also mostly cook with wood and charcoal. The more forest that disappears, the more the lemurs are in trouble. The Lemur Conservation Network hopes that as tourists come to see lemurs in their natural habitat, local people will benefit from tourism more than hunting and farming, and the lemurs may have a future.

Up until then, during two months I'd seen only ring-tailed lemur. In one day there I saw six different species. Here the lemurs were protected and had learned not to be afraid of humans, which meant I got a good view before they launched themselves from tree to tree to get away, or shimmied their way up into the canopy. The sifaka lemur was hilariously distinctive, like a monkey wearing a white fur coat with round, staring yellow eyes, a comical way of leaping about, and a high-pitched call like the sound you make when you hold two blades of grass together and blow air through them. It was hard to believe that the national park was also home to 143 species of frog endemic to that area. I hadn't yet seen any frogs so I asked Jenn, the head of conservation at ValBio, to point one out. When she pointed one out, I still couldn't see it. It was completely camouflaged by the brown leaf it sat upon.

Jenn, who came from Canada, took me around to see all the wildlife, and told me what the centre was doing to protect the rainforest, help regenerate the endangered species, and educate kids while helping the locals. For me, after a good month or so in the wild, it was good to have a bit of banter with native English speakers, Jenn and her students. That was something I missed, however well I got along with Mi.

In the evening, Mi said he wanted to take me to the hot springs. I had visions of a wild pool in the forest, which sounded amazing. In fact we had to pay to get in to a busy swimming pool with hot spring water filtered in, which brought back funny memories of being a lifeguard back in Wales – not quite as natural as I'd expected. But it was a nice place to relax, ready for food and sleep. Because Ranomafana was geared for eco-tourism, the prices were higher than I was used to, and I couldn't eat into the funds too much.

The experience had been great for seeing wildlife and learning about the conservation work, as well as a quick binge of Western food and company. I was pleased to be able to help spread the word, and happy to crack on.

***

Often the locals we came across were shocked to learn that I was walking from the southern point of their country to the northern point, taking in the highest peaks along the way. Many villagers didn't know where Cap Sainte Marie was, so I had to say I'd walked from Fort-Dauphin. People continued to be completely unreliable when we asked how far a village was – some would say 7km, others 10km or 5km – so we stopped asking. Some said it wasn't safe to be walking at night. But people say that the world over. I wondered what they meant was dangerous, since the roads weren't nearly as busy as they'd been in Vietnam, where we'd cycled through the night. Mi got scared and listened hard to warnings, but the Malagasy I'd met seemed to be quite frightened people. I had things still to learn, I was sure.

From time to time we'd arrive at a village to loads of kids screaming and shouting. Some would demand, "Give me your money, white man!" The villages often had no food and it was harder and harder to camp as the land was always owned by someone who wanted to charge us, and there would be kids watching and laughing as we set up the tent. I was confused when some people were mean or nasty in response to a simple smile and greeting. In town, I'd been walking past a group of boys aged around 17 or 18 when one of them raised a stick at me, trying to make me flinch; I raised my fist at him and he flinched, making his friends laugh at him. Five minutes later, a guy walked in front of me with his newborn baby and brought me to a halt; I didn't know what was going on so I just smiled at the little one, but the man gestured that I should give him food. I said I didn't have anything, and went to walk on, but he grabbed my arm to pull me back. I knew my walk across their country wasn't much help to the people I came across, except for the little I spent, though I was hoping it would help to draw other foreigners to Madagascar, which might help some locals to earn a living in the long run. These people weren't to know that – all they saw was a foreigner traipsing through their village.

Once, we'd had a long day of walking and had trouble finding a place to camp with access to clean water. So we came upon a few huts and as it was getting dark and about to rain, we asked if we could camp in the field, and if they would cook for us, which we'd pay for. They said yes; but after we'd finished setting up the tent, they said we also had to pay 10,000 ariary for security and 6,000 for the wood as well as the 3,000 for cooking. This was a lot of money, and I was surprised and angry. We had to pay because it was throwing it down with rain. I ate my rice and noodles in my tent and had an awful night's sleep – dogs barking loudly throughout the night.

We stopped in the town of Ambositra for the day, a place with bigger buildings and rickshaws and markets, and I got a nice clean shave. I had breakfast at the hotel and the staff started to ask about my walk, why I was doing it. Mi had been telling people he was missing his family and wanted to go home. When the staff found I was filming the journey they seemed more curious, so I showed them a TV interview and they were amazed, asking if I was famous. No, I said, but there were people interested in following my progress. They went on the computer, looked at my website and videos, and their attitude changed. Yesterday they were rude and charging me for ketchup, now extremely nice – bit of shame, but that's sometimes how it works. They looked at my Muay Thai video and decided that I had lost an awful amount of weight.

Mi had a drink that morning. He got me anxious when we arrived in villages as he'd sneak off to get a few free shots of rum, and then he wouldn't be focused for planning the next section. We stocked up on food because we'd have several days in the bush now, heading for our next goal: to climb Mount Ibity.

The terrain from here was hilly and lush with rivers, and we were in a good mood when we arrived at the village that served as base camp for the mountain and heard traditional Malagasy music being played. Local people were playing instruments, singing and dancing around the fire. Then I noticed a group of older Westerners taking photos and joining in, and I realised this was set up by a tour operator; all the times I'd seen this sort of thing, the locals were just doing it for themselves. I'd found myself on the tourist route for a moment, but it was a pleasant surprise to see a generator for electricity, which possibly meant a fridge with cold drinks.

The next morning we got the bad news: we needed to buy a permit because the mountain was privately owned. Mi went to talk to the local family who "owned" the mountain. I didn't like the idea of having to pay to climb a mountain; there was so little free, wild land here, unlike Mongolia. We'd thought Mount Ibity was in the national park, but it now turned out we could only climb it if we paid 45,000 ariary, and because of my continual effort to curb spending, I didn't have extra cash on me. After checking that there was no chance of getting any cash nearby, I realised we'd have to walk to Antsirabe, the nearest city about 30km away, just to use the ATM. And then walk back again to climb the mountain.

Rather than moaning about the situation, I just had to crack on and deal with it, and I drew on the frustration to provide me with energy, just as I had when the malaria nearly forced me to give up the expedition. If we had to walk a full day to get money to pay to walk a mountain, we'd do it! I had to persevere. It's not a challenge until something goes wrong. And when you feel like you're falling flat on your face, it's your chance to shine. When we finally set off to climb Ibity we left our bags behind for the day and hired a local guide, who said if we were fast we'd do it in ten hours.

It was a beautiful day, hot with a slight breeze, and we walked quickly, determined, though we took the time to notice ruins of Malagasy houses built over 300 years ago; we picked fruit to eat and ventured a little way inside a cave whose end nobody had ever discovered. The guide pointed out spiky-leaved aloe plants, of which there are about a dozen species on Ibity. I broke off a stem and rubbed the fluid into my chapped, sunburned lips to soothe and heal them. As we climbed through the rock-strewn landscape, I enjoyed the freedom of trekking without a heavy bag and decided to take the next day off to post off some kit I didn't need for the next section. I'd also go to the national parks office to double-check whether the mountains I was aiming to climb later were privately owned or free to climb.

The top of Mount Ibity levels out and it's not immediately obviously where the summit is. We started celebrating only to realise the peak 50 metres away was higher. The hour-long scramble involved quite a lot of rock climbing, but we made it to the summit and then down the steep slope and back to the village. I had summited the third of the eight highest mountains in Madagascar, one of my major goals as I made my way north on foot, and it felt good. I was now into the true heart of the expedition.

In the morning, Mi came to my room, looking anxious – it looked as if he'd been crying most of the night and hadn't slept. He said his son was ill with malaria and his wife had been panicking and calling him all night. It was a shock. I told him to go home straight away and make sure he was getting all the right treatment. I paid him there and then so he had the money to get there, saw him off on the bus and wished him the best for his son. Mi and I had really connected, in spite of my frustration with him when he drank. He had been like a brother to me out there. I organised for Joe to come to meet me, and spent the rest of the day catching up with my parents and with business.

Joe arrived in the evening, and we set out the next morning, straight into the bush on small tracks. We stopped at a small village and headed for the small hut serving food, just to ask for directions and rest for a minute. The people seemed to make jokes about me to get a laugh out of their friends. I knew it shouldn't bother me, but in the heat when you're hungry and thirsty and tired, it doesn't take long for things to get to you. It made me all the more grateful for the people who went out of their way to be hospitable and friendly, trying out their first ever words of English to talk to me. We came across groups of kids heading home from school on their lunch break; once they saw me they ran away. It was great to see their energy, but a shame they were scared of white people.

We were aiming for Famoizankova, at 2,367 metres the first of three high peaks on this stretch from Antsirabe to Antananarivo. We were now following the spine of the island. We walked into mountains covered by pine forest, and reached the first summit later that day. For these days we would stay on high ground and camp along the way, wherever we could find water. Trying to find a way forward, we hacked our way through the forest, with a sheer drop right beside us. It was getting reckless but we had to find a camping spot before it got dark. The mountains continued in all directions and the small unmarked tracks were sometimes tough to find. Luckily, with a lot of cuts and bruises, we made it to flatter ground just as the light faded completely. It was cold, so we got our woolly hats and gloves out.

That next morning it was freezing when we woke high in the mountains, but it wasn't a bad feeling to be so cold after such a long time in hot temperatures. My tent was wet from condensation that dripped onto my sleeping bag. We packed up and left fast, with another mountain to climb: Inanobe at 2,325 metres. We walked over paddy fields and hills and bridges made from simple tree trunks; Madagascar often felt like an obstacle course.

A guy shouted, "Oi, white person, just crossed my field!"

Joe laughed and said, "Yes! So?"

"Do you have security with you?"

"We don't need security!" shouted Joe, and the guy left.

Joe and I were getting on well, telling stories and having a laugh as we walked. We had good energy going. When we came across illegal loggers cutting down trees – deforestation is such a big problem in Madagascar – Joe shouted, "You shouldn't be here, this is illegal!" We heard them throw down their tools and drive away. We'd scared them off.

Stopping to eat, we were directed to a path that the locals said should take us to the top of the mountain. We found our way and began to scramble up the cliff; we were out of breath, still exhausted from yesterday's climb, but we persevered and made it. It was beautiful, flat and grassy on top with pine trees. And we could now see the third and final mountain before Antananarivo. It looked far away, with plenty of peaks in between, but with no time to waste we continued. We came across a family and asked them for directions. They said it was tough, and added that I should be careful as there were people on top that had been killing white people. I hoped they were massively mistaken.

The next morning, the mountains ahead looked intimidating as we hunted for Mount Tsiafajavona. We asked more locals and they said it took them around a day to a day and a half to get there, which was bad news because they walked fast with no heavy bags. I expected it would take us two days. It was a hot morning and we climbed up and down, up and down, on messy tracks that went here and there. But the scenery was stunning, valley after valley, mountain after mountain with quaint little villages, the land often stripped of trees and smooth with low grass.

Joe went ahead and approached a village where everyone was outside going about their business, chickens and dogs and fires going. When we both arrived there was nothing but the dogs and the chickens, and smoke coming out of the windows; everyone had run away. Joe called out to say we meant no harm, but it was deserted. Just one old guy, working on his wooden cart, was friendly. I gave him a big smile to show I wasn't hostile, and we asked him why people were running away – this wasn't the first time people had fled when they saw me. He told us that in the 1960s white people, especially the French who ruled the island then, walked through the country with guns and sometimes treated the Malagasy with brutality. So people who had never seen a Westerner before – because it was now rare to see white people walking in the bush – believed that all white people were bad guys out to hurt them, and they panicked and ran for safety. Some believed that white people stole their organs. It was amazing to encounter such beliefs so close to the capital city. I was glad to have learned something.

When I had said we would get all three mountains done in three days, Joe had said it was impossible. As we searched for the right mountain peak to climb, my GPS was telling me one thing and the locals were telling us another. I didn't use the GPS much, but it was always good to check it. Every time we summited a mountain, we could see a bigger one in the distance. It wasn't promising.

The highest peaks had sacrifice areas on top. To honour their ancestors and gain their favour, the Malagasy people would sacrifice livestock. Slaughtering a valuable zebu, worth more than an average monthly salary, would keep the ancestors happy, especially useful if you were getting married or building a house. So the summits of the highest mountains had blood-stained rocks, sometimes with a low wall around. Joe said he was sure from this which peak was the right one – yet my GPS was telling me differently. It was frustrating and I could tell Joe was knackered and just wanted to get it done and go back down. But I stressed how important it was that I hit the correct summit.

"No, this isn't it – that one's the peak," he said.

When we got to where he said we should be, we could see that it clearly wasn't the highest peak. And when he saw that he threw his bag down in a sulk. I went back down the mountain so I could walk up to the other peak. I noticed that as the walking got to

Joe, he became more stressed and moody, and he'd argue with me on every point, when there was no need – we were in it as a team and should have been helping each other. When he was convinced he was right about something, there was no telling him otherwise. He'd say, "There's 2.6 kilometres in one mile," and he'd be adamant that he was right. After research confirmed there were 1.6 kilometres in a mile, he still wasn't having it. Mostly I just bit my tongue.

We did manage to do all three peaks in three days, as I'd hoped, in spite of his ridiculing the idea. So when I said we'd get to Tana the next day, and he replied, "Don't be stupid," I finally flipped. But we cleared the air after a lot of petty argument, which was good. We had successfully summited the three mountains together.

On the way to "Tana" (Antananarivo), he wanted to stop at the home of some friends who he said were like family; they turned out to be the people who helped him get off the streets and gave him money to start up. They invited me in and gave us some cold juice. They started lifting our bags before we set off again and laughed at how light Joe's was compared to mine – they were messing around, slapping his cap down.

Tana, the capital of the island, is a sprawling city and even from the outskirts it would take around five hours to get to the centre. So when we got to the outskirts and spotted a pizza restaurant, we went straight in and got ourselves a huge pizza each and a giant banana smoothie and ice cream for dessert. Having all that food inside us, a big change from all that rice and sugar tea, we were laughing and giggling, the tensions behind us. We continued into the city, hiding inside a pharmacy when a massive thunderstorm hit, the biggest I'd seen so far in the country. Everyone was taking cover as the roads were flooded and turned into rivers. Joe was scared we'd be hit by lightning.

"It doesn't look like the rain is stopping," I said finally. "Shall we just crack on? At least there's hardly any traffic!"

Joe didn't fancy it. "Let's get a taxi," he said, thinking we were in for a miserable few hours in pelting rain. "We've made it to the city."

"I'm not getting a taxi! We walk right to the doorstep of the place that we're sleeping." This was still part of the adventure.

I put my waterproof jacket on – uselessly, I admit – and off we went, wading through knee-high water in places. People were sinking into ditches, unable to see the way. But the people sheltering in doorways would shout out encouragement as they watched me walking past with my rucksack on. I said goodbye to Joe as he went to his house, and I went to stay with Gilles.

At Gilles's place in Tana, I spent half the night trying to kill all the mosquitoes that landed on my ear every time I almost dropped off to sleep. Some places had mosquito nets, or netting on the windows, but Gilles's home was not one of them. And as for the noise in the morning in the city... I just wasn't used to it after so long in the bush. I moved to a hotel so I could get some work done – preparing kit, going over maps, backing up film footage and photos, and sending footage to the production company in the UK.

My next guide would be Max, head guide of Madamax, a real bush man but well educated too. I was very much looking forward to trekking with him. I could tell Gilles didn't want to let him go –

I'd almost destroyed Joe and Mi with the walking. Max and I met to discuss the way forward.

I had already covered more than half the country as the crow flies, but the next weeks would be extremely challenging – more than I realised. There would be rivers to contend with, and the weather would be different, with the rainy season beginning also. Max told me we'd be in jungle more often than not, and the peaks were higher and much harder to climb than in the south. I had a few mountains to tackle in this last, long section north, including Maromokotro, the highest at 2,876 metres. There would be fewer people around, especially in remote Antsiranana province. We might walk for ten days or more without seeing anyone, and would be living off the land, using bushcraft and survival skills.

From what he told me, it sounded as though I was about to embark on a brand new expedition. My excitement and motivation came flooding back. We sharpened our machetes. I was ready.

# 11: Tana to Bealanana: into the jungle

As Max and I walked out of the city centre, we picked up the newspaper to see ourselves in it. We stopped for some breakfast and the owner wanted to have his photo taken with us. It was a hot day as we hit the trail, and the first few hours after leaving the city behind were busy. We both soon had blisters, breaking back into the swing of things after over a week off. But we seemed to have bonded and it felt as though we were old friends, the hours flying by as we chatted.

We left behind the national road, where vehicles were constantly beeping at us and getting too close for comfort, and headed onto smaller and smaller paths leading from village to village, into hills and thick forest. At around 1,500 metres it was beautiful and fresh, good to be back in the bush. We found ourselves some tea leaves and raspberry bushes, and had a hook with a line for fishing. When we stopped for lunch at a small village, two young boys watched me, so, since I still had signal on my phone I showed them a clever trick with a video, where you tilt the iPhone 360° to see film from all over the world. They couldn't believe it: it was amazing to show them Arctic kayaking and Mongolian nomads with their eagles.

We took a rest at an empty spot in the forest, which Max told me was a "men's market" where local guys meet every week to sell super-strong rum. It's illegal, and the police come, but only to take some as a 'fine' when they catch people. We saw a man cutting down trees, and Max confronted him, asking why he was doing that when his sons would grow up without forest. He said he was forced to do it to make a living in order to survive, and they'd then grow rice in the paddy fields to sell for food.

The views were stunning: a vast wooded and mountainous landscape, with a river running through the middle of a deep valley. We came to our first river crossing, the colour of strong milky tea with deep green foliage trailing down the banks and gentle hills all around. Since there was no bridge or canoe, we waded across; it was only up to our knees and we had a quick wash once we reached the other side. Every now and then we'd pass someone and exchange *"Salaama"* or hello, maybe ask for information on where the next water was. At a village, a local guy who'd been walking alongside us earlier provided us with a pot and wood so we could cook ourselves some noodles and tea. The next big river came up to our bellybuttons as we waded in, so we had to strip off. Apparently there were crocodiles in this river – further down the river, but there's nothing like knowing there are crocodiles around to keep you alert.

When a big rainstorm hit, we stopped by a small hut for tea. The lady owner was impressed with what I was doing, and gave me some bananas to take with me. Two teenage girls we met along the way found it hilarious that we were walking to the north, and we took a photo of them wearing our rucksacks. We continued down a wide open sandy track, which was easy to follow so Max and I could chat away about family, life and whatever popped into our heads. Other times we just walked and thought, listening to the noises of nature with mountains and trees around us, and a dark blue rain cloud just far enough away. Flooded paddy fields reflected the sky, and we found a Giant Comet moth – bigger than my hand and kite-shaped, with bright yellow patterned wings.

Sometimes people would walk with us to their village and invite us in, give us food and water and then wave us off. Then a guy riding a bike stopped to tell us there had been a shooting at the next village, two bandits with Kalashnikovs, one man shot dead. It turned out they were ex-military, not zebu bandits but there to steal money. A girl said her father was shot and killed only three months before at the same village. We decided to make a detour; we were thirsty but kept our heads down and powered on forwards. When we met the mayor of another village, he said the gunmen had been found and taken to prison. Max showed people the newspaper article that we were both in, and they gave us a room to stay in that night – just a small room with rat droppings on my bed, but we avoided the rain.

We reached the town of Ambatondrazaka and since Max was going through the normal suffering while getting used to the walking, we decided to stay at a hotel. I found a little restaurant and said I'd come back the next morning to treat myself to a bowl of Coco Pops. I arrived in the morning, starving and fixated on the idea of a bowl of my favourite cereal with nice, cold milk. It took ages for them to bring first the bowl, and then a spoon, and finally the milk – but it was boiling hot. I had a little tantrum – I'd been so looking forward to my Coco Pops, and now they'd ruined it! They said I could just wait for it to cool down. But I didn't want to wait, and I couldn't bear the idea of warm milk on a hot day. Then Max explained. In a place like this, it wasn't as though they had just poured the milk from a two-pint carton in the fridge. They'd actually had to milk the zebu, and then boil the milk to kill the bacteria. I felt like such an idiot and had to laugh at myself for going on a strop. How we take our modern conveniences for granted.

As we left town, Max and I heard our favourite Malagasy song playing on someone's radio. It was such an upbeat song that it instantly lifted our spirits and brought a huge smile to our faces. We sang and danced to it as we walked.

Little communities of huts with tall grass-thatched roofs sat in small clearings on the hillsides, the land stretching off forever in steep, bush-covered hills and deep river valleys. The walls of the huts were often plastered with cracked mud, the same red colour as the ground. Some sections of hillside were densely wooded, others had been burned down. One day we heard Christmas songs blaring out from a hut, and it made me wonder what my family and friends were doing. Some days went painfully slowly; my bag felt heavy again, and with my loss of weight and strength I struggled.

I took my mind off things by asking Max about the customs and rituals of Madagascar. In the old days, when the man of the family died, it was tradition to destroy everything, burn down the huts, kill the zebu, leaving the family with nothing. It wasn't usually done any more, but they still had fascinating rituals when it came to their relationship with the dead. Every two to seven years during the dry season, people took the bones of their ancestors out of the family crypt for "the turning of the bones", *famadihana*, followed by a celebration with feasting and dancing to show their ongoing love for those who had passed away.

We stopped at a place in the shade, and the girl there wanted to be a guide so she had lots of questions for Max. The people gave us a small fish each. Having finished eating I put my bowl on the floor, which the lady took, then I put the spoon on the floor.

Max panicked and said, "No, that's a taboo, it's forbidden."

The Malagasy way is to eat from the spoon, give it one dip in water then pass it on to the next person. But the people weren't offended – they smiled, nodding, understanding that I was only just learning about their culture.

In the heat and humidity of this forested region heading north, I reached the 100th day of my expedition. I hadn't been walking every one of the 100 days as I'd stopped to recover from malaria and to meet the conservation people and so on, but it was great to be at this point. Yet two days later, I found myself quite emotional, lacking in motivation. I didn't have any doubts that I'd make it but I wasn't enjoying it. It was hard to explain why, as the terrain was beautiful. I was probably just mentally and physically drained after 100 days of challenges, constantly alert and worrying about what obstacle might be next. It was hard to simply enjoy the moment. It felt as though the true Ash Dykes wasn't here and I had to wait for him to return. I put it down to missing family, friends and general comfort. I had taken a beating every day for a while.

As if to add insult to injury, it started throwing it down with rain that day, so we put our waterproofs on, cold and wet, expecting a miserable night. Within an hour, we came across a mountain village; everyone was inside sheltering from the rain, but when we knocked on a hut, a lady and her younger sister answered, inviting us in to dry off. We had a hot drink and then both slumped down and fell asleep. Maybe my mood had been mostly down to fatigue. The women looked after us, prepared us food and gave us a room to sleep in. It was truly appreciated and warming to see the way people worked together to help one another here. What seemed like a daunting challenge in an environment with no electricity was made easier when tackled as a team. I felt humbled to witness it. This raised my spirits a little. I reminded myself that like them, Max and I had to continue working as a team to overcome all obstacles thrown our way. Rather than looking too far ahead and worrying about all that lay in the way, we'd have to take each challenge as it came – day by day. Losing motivation is a horrible thing; you think all sorts of thoughts about your life; but also you have to remember it's a phase and fight through it. I wasn't out of it yet, but this had helped.

Paths led us around endless paddy fields and over marsh land where I'd constantly lose my shoe. On one river crossing I fell, my leg muscles giving way under the weight, and I just managed to save my bag as I slipped. I worried about the expensive electronic equipment; it was in dry bags but after 100 days I wondered how protected they were. One day as we walked across big empty hills, dark rain clouds gathered around us. It seemed the eye of the storm was directly above us as we stood at the highest point for miles around. The heavens opened and we were hit by hail, probably due to the altitude. The winds drove it into our faces. As in the Mongolian sandstorms, we just had to keep our heads down and crack on forwards. After a cold and wet night, having woken up hungry as it had been raining so hard when we camped, we woke to an eerily misty morning.

Somewhere across the huge hills, swampland and rivers ahead, our map told us there was a village. We set out gamely, but before long we found ourselves at the edge of a big pond or flooded field and had to double-back. This happened over and over, as if we were on an extended assault course, always with something else to come. The motivation really wasn't there, but it was discipline that made me keep going. At one point on a riverbank I slipped and landed on concrete – painful, but at least I hadn't landed in the water. The village seemed to have vanished so we decided we had to stop and cook noodles to get some food inside us. The next village a few hours later also seemed to have vanished, which was slightly worrying as I only had one more ration pack to share between us and nothing else. We set up camp.

We woke up next morning to the beautiful, freaky cries and howls of lemurs echoing all around us – different families, different species. We stood looking out into the forest. They were hidden, but the noises were mesmerising.

Then, to our surprise, someone walked past. This was our chance to ask about food and the next village. He said the next village was a two-hour walk away and we must take water from the river as there was no other water source. We came across two more locals who gave us doughnuts and cigarettes for Max – so his spirits lifted massively.

We made it to this tiny village, the first in many days. The huts blended into the red earth of the hillside, and women carried their loads of washing on their heads. It was quiet and there was no food to buy but a lady said she could cook us noodles. After this stop I felt motivated again; my mood simply felt lifted, and I put that chapter behind me, looking forward to the next.

At the next village, after a demanding walk up and down, around and over hills, as a huge rain cloud was coming in, a family allowed us to stay with them. The houses in this region had grass walls and roofs, and the main streets were wide sandy tracks. All of us sat round on a candlelit floor and dug into rice, noodles and some greens. It was their first time having a *fazah* as a guest, and we all enjoyed it. When we slept, I had four kids on the floor next to me, then the adults and baby in the bed, but I was happy to be dry and inside.

We set off with some bananas, marching through the loud, humid jungle – the scream of insects was ear-piercing. Max spotted a small fossa, a type of wild cat. Lemurs were screaming and howling their different sounds – the fossa is their main natural predator – and it was beautiful to hear nature and nothing else. The bugs and butterflies came in all colours and sizes, some huge. I felt like I was in the *Avatar* movie. When we got to a viewpoint and looked down, there was a stunning vista of a valley dense with lush green jungle and a wide river winding through it. We'd been melting with the heat but by sunset it was raining lightly. We threw rocks up at mango trees to knock the fruit down. When we found a place to sleep, the insects were so big that I could hear them crawling around.

It was Christmas Eve when we crossed a river on a bridge that was almost submerged, and arrived at a small village full of friendly people and over-excited children. The guy who owned the local shop invited us in to stay at his family's house. We relaxed inside, and a ton of kids poked their head through the door to get a close view of me. Max told them to go away as they were blocking our breeze, but I occasionally went outside to see them, putting tinsel around me. The people truly made me feel at home; the lady of the house said she would sleep in another part of the house so I could have a bed. There was barely any electricity, maybe just a single solar panel, so it was dark inside and we sat around in candlelight drinking tea and learning about one another. I gave them some of my chicken tikka masala ration pack to try – the man of the house loved it but the others weren't too sure.

The Malagasy would usually go to sleep around 9pm but that night the family went out to sing carols with the whole village. This was a traditional Malagasy Christmas. Max and I stayed in the house to rest, but the enthusiastic singing went on at great volume until after midnight, when the noise was replaced by snoring. It was an experience I won't forget. After a few hours' sleep, we set off walking early in the morning, wishing everyone a merry Christmas.

The day was cloudy, perfect for walking, but there were more than 15 rivers, each of which took at least 10 minutes to cross by the time we'd taken off our shoes and dried out. It was strange there weren't more bridges, as the routes were well used by locals. The hills were tough, and the forest humid. I climbed a mango tree to get a few fruit down – mango was perfect for walking and eating, and it gave me something to do along the way. I ran out of fresh water for a good few hours, so drained the juice from mangoes until we made it to a village with a clean river running through, and pitched up on a field. It was a beautiful evening. The local people at first just stared from a distance; then suddenly they were bringing us mangoes and lychees and wood. It was amazing to be welcomed. For me, cooking in the evening when camping was a great part of the day – to feel good, after covering a good distance, and looking forward to a great night's sleep, protected by my tent from the insects and the rats.

The next day dawned with the village in mist and a dark blue sky lit still by an almost full moon. We started with a hot and steep climb up the mountains, which instantly made us sweat, but I loved it. I realised if I wore just sandals on my feet, then the river crossings were easier as I could wade straight through. When the way was muddy from rain, sometimes a sandal would get sucked down and it was tough to pull back out without losing balance and falling in completely. Once we crossed a wide, deep river on a narrow walkway that was completely underwater and invisible. If we had fallen in, we'd have been heading for the rapids. But gradually, over these few weeks heading north, I got used to all the rivers and actually enjoyed them. They were beautiful, the colour of milky tea with sandy banks, the forest coming almost down to the shore, and green hills in the distance. We were on a roll, walking and walking and barely stopping. I came across three big snakes, each about a metre and a half long – but so far, no crocodiles.

New Year's Eve was a good one, relaxing and getting things organised in a town called Antsakabary, with sandy tracks for roads. The houses were a mix of wood and mud-brick, and the long eaves of neat metal roofs propped up on wooden stilts. All around here, the mountains stretched off into the distance, carpeted in green.

I spent the day eating a lot, drying out kit, washing clothes and clearing my bag of rubbish. The food was nice and cheap. Max went out to check out the celebrations but we agreed it was best for me to stay in as it could get quite rowdy with a lot of drinking. I was happy to get an early night. We had some big scrambles ahead of us if we wanted to get to Bealanana in two days, the challenge we'd set ourselves; I didn't know if it was possible but having a challenge kept me energised, and I was raring to get going. Bealanana was so close to the northern tip of the island, looking at a map.

Once we arrived there, things would change again as we'd be joined by Suzanna and Liva. Suzanna was a girl I'd met just a couple of days after completion of the Mongolia expedition, in Ulaanbaatar. She was there doing a project with the eagle hunters in the west, so she wanted to ask me and Rob, my logistics manager, for tips and advice. She'd now agreed to join our expedition as a professional photographer.

Liva, like Max, worked as a guide for Gilles at Madamax. He joined us to help Suzanna carry her heavy equipment – electronics and camera kit, which I knew she wouldn't be able to handle alone, as well as her food and other camping kit, over the next section that we'd be trekking together in jungle and mountains. Liva and Suzanna had met up in Tana, and would be driving with Max's wife in the 4x4 to meet us in Bealanana. Liva couldn't speak much English but he knew French, and Suzanna was fluent in French, so they could communicate.

I was excited about their joining us, and about getting the final small section done. It seemed the expedition was in the bag, that this was the home stretch, over 75 percent of the way through, just four or five weeks left.

Max went quiet when I said that to him. "Don't jinx it. This next section's going to be really tough."

We'd be trekking up mountains in the rainy season, the edge of the cyclone season in fact. The tracks were getting muddier and tougher. I had no idea what was to come. The next couple of days to Bealanana gave me a taster, as if to mock my bravado.

There was still music playing at 5am when I woke, but I love music and was full of the energy of the new year. We got a soya tea and set off. Within the first five minutes we had to cross a river then spent the rest of the morning climbing a mountain so steep that we hung our shirts on trees to dry the sweat off before pushing on again. The paths then dropped down and led us through grass taller than us, across a big river where the sinking mud sucked us down – then we found out we'd gone the wrong way and had to go back across again. With that and dodging falling mangoes, it was bonkers. But that night was a clear one and the stars were unbelievable.

The locals here were used to walking. They'd walk a whole day to the market once a week, then stay the night, get what they need to last them for a week and walk all the way back again. But the next day was beyond even our expectations. We walked for 15 hours – and the last five of them were in the dark.

We crossed disused paddy fields that were just bog land. We took off what clothes we could and waded through the deep mud in bare feet, seeing the way with a head torch. Every other step we went down into the mud up to our waists, just about keeping our balance as we became weighed down with mud. I couldn't fall in with all my electronics in my bag. It was hellish. We'd ascertained that we were heading the right way but there was no sign of life up ahead – it felt like the middle of nowhere. Spikes and thorns under the mud stuck into our feet; we were covered in cuts and our legs were cramping up. Eventually we heard the generator of the village, but it was still so far away. We were both exhausted and in bad moods with no patience for finding the path, so we cut straight across the paddy fields, losing sandals, breaking sandals; we crossed a part where we were walking through human sewage. Dogs ran up, growling, looking as if they wanted to attack us. We just shouted back at them.

When we arrived at the guest house in Bealanana, our clothes were ripped and we were covered in mud and worse. The only thing to eat was rice and processed cheese slices, so that's what we had, and we showered off. The next day the others would arrive and we would push on, across the three last mountains, all the way to the northern tip of Madagascar.

# 12: To Cap D'Ambre: rivers, leeches and Gertrude the cockerel

In Bealanana the following evening, the street lights and the Malagasy music playing gave the place a party atmosphere. Suzanna was excited about joining us, and I loved catching up with a friend. We all sat outside at a barbecue place, eating and getting on well. Max and I told them about the previous day's walking and they laughed and said it sounded hideous. Liva, a short guy but always ripped from all his training, was in a typically good mood. I knew he was reliable and that I'd be able to count on him.

I sat back, feeling both humble and proud that by the age of 25 I'd managed to plan a world-first expedition, and had successfully organised bringing Suzanna and Liva all the way to this tiny place whilst trekking through such difficult situations. I was excited about the team. To top it all off, I had a phone call from my dad saying he and my uncle Luke had booked to come to Madagascar when I finished. I was loving my life, and too buzzed about everything to sleep much that night.

We set out and started getting into the swing of things. The locals had managed to fix my broken sandal. Suzanna started getting footage and photos. On the first night when we all crammed into a hut to sleep, there was a big spider, about half the size of my hand, and Suzanna wouldn't let us rest until we'd chased it out.

The first hiccup came at Mangindrano, the last settlement where we'd have chance to stock up on food before the mountains. We thought it would be a quick and easy stop of an hour or so, but the trouble came with the national parks access that we'd need to summit the final mountain of the expedition, Maromokotro, although we had two to go before we reached it. The officials told us that this entrance to the national park was for research and science purposes only, and that in order to have climbing access, we'd have to go back to Antananarivo and get a stamp and letter of invitation from the national parks authority. There were no trucks or roads around here and it had taken me and Max a month to walk from Tana. We obviously weren't going to walk back just to get that piece of paper. We weren't turning back for anyone, in fact.

We tried everything. We phoned the tourism office and they said they couldn't help, which annoyed me because they were part of the team and had previously granted us access to all the national parks. Gilles argued with them down the phone but he couldn't sort anything either. The whole plan had been in place for over eight months and everyone was aware of it, so if a permit was needed it should have been sorted out. I was fuming.

The next morning, with no one able to help, we decided just to go for it anyway. I wasn't risking the expedition for a permit. We told the office that we wouldn't be entering the national park. We'd only be in there for a day or two anyway, as it was only the peak of Maromokotro that was in national park land. It was nerve-wracking for Max, who had visions of us being dragged back by a man with a gun. But I reckoned we had to crack on.

But before we left, we had one more thing to arrange. The locals said we must take a white cockerel with us to the peak of the highest mountain, Maromokotro – we made sure the national parks officer didn't see it – as it would keep the bad spirits away from us in the forest as we summited the mountain. We had to take it from here as there wouldn't be any more communities with white chickens from here on in.

We got one, a shy little guy, and I named him Gertrude. So Gertrude would have to come with us for the two mountains prior to Maromokotro also – for the next two to three weeks – and we'd have to release him alive on the peak of Maromokotro as a sacrifice. We also had to take a small bottle of rum and a tub of honey; on the peak of the mountain we had to mix the two together and take a shot, so the bad spirits would allow us back down safely.

We had Gertrude, we had rum, we had honey, and off we went. I kept Gertrude in my hands – it was too hot for him to go in the top pouch of my rucksack. He was about a foot tall when standing straight, but slender and light. Everyone gathered around us – I think they'd liked our company – and they all waved us off as we walked towards the mountains, starting with Ambohimirahavavy.

It was the rainy season now and the rivers were bigger, the

ground even marshier. But we were excited and ploughed on through. A local was heading in the same direction and told us to follow him to a bamboo shelter where he lived with his wife and son, and to eat something as there was nothing beyond. He showed us how to collect tobacco leaves, heat them near the fire, crush them and mix them with ash from the fire then rub it on our skin to keep the leeches away. We gathered a tubful and the guy directed us up the ridge through the jungle and wished us the best of luck.

From there I took the lead, machete in hand, hacking a path through the bush. It was steep and densely covered in jungle, the most difficult climb I'd had so far by a long way, but the rufus lemurs were howling away and leaping about above us in the trees. It took an age to get anywhere at all. We slowed down even more when surrounded by dead bamboo, where it took half a dozen thwacks with the machete to get through each stem. We didn't look at the compass for a while, and realised we'd done a complete loop on ourselves.

We covered just over five miles in the whole day. It was draining, to say the least. It was dark and we couldn't find water, so we'd have to hack down enough bamboo to set up camp, and risk using up the water from the bottles we'd brought.

"Tomorrow is another day," I said, joking, to Max and he laughed. It was becoming almost a catchphrase.

We kept Gertrude safe on a length of string tied to a tree. Suzanna and I decided to sit outside and eat, until we saw a dozen leeches crawling towards us. We looked down at ourselves and we had half a dozen already on us. Suzanna screamed and we retreated to our tents. Gertrude ended up taking shelter on top of my tent.

The next day, we tried everything to get to the peak of the mountain, but it seemed unreachable. We hacked through all sorts of bush, from the wiry type that trips you up, gets caught around your ankles and holds you down, to trees with big leaves that stick in your face and sharp new bamboo spearing up through the ground. It was battering the hell out of us. We had to keep our distance so we weren't hit in the face by branches as the person in front passed through. We had to watch out for the leeches which dropped onto us from the trees above, and take our packs off to tunnel through the bamboo. We pulled our bodies up cliff faces, using trees as hand holds.

I'd hit at the jungle with my machete as I marched, shouting at the flies... *Damn you, Madagascar – you won't beat me!* It was stupid, but the anger helped to keep me going. Sometimes I'd film myself taking my anger out this way, and I'd look at the footage that night and consider deleting it. But I always kept it.

We tried so many options, to go up and over the mountain, to follow it round, or to go down to the river. We just didn't know what to do or which way to go any more. We were losing hope. We stopped and put the packs down to figure out what next. We'd been battling for hours but were only a few hundred metres from where we'd woken up that morning.

We decided to try one last time, going around the ridge rather than directly up. After hacking through the bush and covering a grand total of a mile and a half in six hours, we eventually reached what looked as though it might be the summit. The lads wanted me to believe it was the summit. I think deep down they knew it wasn't, but they wanted to get off that mountain. But I knew although it had been a difficult day, we had to keep going or I'd feel like I'd cheated myself. I pointed to where the true summit was.

"'Don't give up now. Let's just push on and get it done.'"

So we continued and found a small track, which we followed slowly. It was getting dark when we came across a water source – the water had to be boiled and filtered as there were leeches in it – and decided to set up camp again in the eerie dead bamboo. Three of us would continue while one of us, Liva, stayed behind to boil water and cook. We headed straight up to the summit, and it was amazing to finally hit Ambohimirahavavy at 2,301 metres.

There was nothing to see except mist and thick jungle, with creepers and moss hanging from the branches. I was pretty sure barely anyone climbed to this place, and certainly no Westerner. We went back down and celebrated around the camp fire. But in my tent later, I wondered nervously about the next mountain, Andohanisambirano (otherwise known as just Sambirano). Tomorrow was another day.

But the next day was much the same – trying everything to get to the second mountain. We found our way down to a river, filled our bottles and considered two paths, one upstream and one up the mountain. I favoured the first but the lads the second, so off we went up the mountain. Before we knew it, the path had disappeared and we were hacking through dense jungle again. Every now and then we'd stop, put the bags down, and two of us would go on ahead to search for the path; we developed a whistle call and response so we could find one another again. But it was ridiculously tough and it was getting dark. We'd covered two and a half miles. We were all pretty low, having been in the jungle for three days and covered seven miles. We couldn't go on like this – it would take us weeks and we'd run out of food. We were on a steep incline with nowhere to camp so we turned back to where we'd had lunch, in another bamboo patch that had to be hacked down and flattened in the light of our head-torches. We went to our various tents having eaten nothing but dry noodles.

The next day we went back to the river. The path up the river started out promising, and we felt quite upbeat as we made a fire to cook lunch, fashioning a stand out of bamboo to fit the cooking pot over; but the path started to fade. The locals don't walk the mountains in the rainy season, so the paths grow over again, and I suggested we walk in the river itself. We made better progress for an hour or two, but then the bamboo covered the river, and some parts were much deeper than the rest, the rocks were slippery and the logs were unsafe.

As we continued we noticed the cliffs on either side of us were now as steep as hell directly above us, so there was no trekking up them anymore. Then eventually our nightmare came true: our way was blocked by a waterfall. If I'd been on my own without a bag full of electronics, I'd probably have attempted to climb it, but I had others to think about, including Suzanna, not to mention Gertrude.

We had now exhausted all options except to go back the same way we'd come, including going up and over the eighth highest mountain all over again. At least we had that one well and truly ticked off. It was heartbreaking to go all the way back but we'd gone through all our snacks and if we went back to Mangindrano we could top up on food, reassess our route and maybe find a guide.

We cracked on, stayed positive and made our way back to the river, topping up on water just as a huge storm broke loose. We put our waterproofs on and started trekking up the mountain, stopping over and over to pull off leeches which were washed off the trees by the rain and fell down our tops. We had to keep checking each other and pull off any leeches. Suzanna's waterproof poncho seemed to attract more leeches than anything else and she was covered in them, inside and out, her face bleeding too. Liva and Max were wearing shorts so their legs were dripping blood, and the rain made it even worse. My body was protected but I found a couple crawling on my face and pulled them off.

After a very steep trek for a few hours, we made it to the summit and back to the old camp spot in the bamboo. Somehow, despite everything, we were still all in high spirits, looking forward to Mangindrano recharging our batteries and finding someone who knew the way. Even Gertrude seemed happy sticking with us. He needed us and we needed him.

5.30am: it's bad enough waking up in such cold that you need a woolly hat and gloves; but it's even worse having first to put on wet boxer shorts, socks and trousers.

One biscuit for breakfast and then we continued. I followed my GPS back the same way we came, although in the meantime I found a short cut that reduced four hours' worth of hacking to under 30 minutes. But breaking the trail meant getting soaked to the skin. We worked our way down the slippery steep slopes. Suzanna hated it, constantly slipping and falling, still in pain from a fall two days earlier when she'd narrowly missed a sharp bamboo stalk. We kept a steady pace, with the leeches still attacking us. When it rained, we couldn't be bothered to put waterproofs on. We just wanted to get to Mangindrano. We stopped at the bamboo shelter of the man who had directed us up to the first mountain, and asked if he wanted to guide us up to the second. He seemed unsure.

After eight hours' walking and sinking in mud, we arrived back at Mangindrano in the afternoon. As we made our way into the village, we heard drumming. I was pulled into a room and had a cape wrapped around me, was given a golden goblet with beer inside and given a seat while the local people danced around me in a crazed way, playing their instruments. It was a spirit ritual, where people would call up the spirits by playing music, drinking rum and dancing. It was so loud, and one of the woman was dancing in a freaky way and a man told me there was a spirit inside her. It looked like there were plenty of the other kind of spirits inside half of the people.

We went straight back to our old corner of the village, then to the lady who made banana fritters. Another woman started preparing rice and beans. We hung our kit over the bamboo fences as the late afternoon sun came out from behind the clouds, and went to wash in the river. As usual, I wolfed down so much food; not a good idea after going hungry for days. We laughed about the adventure of the last few days. The jungle had chewed us up and spat us out, but we were heading back for more.

Even more hilarious was the fact that Gertrude had become domesticated and wouldn't leave us alone. We left him at the back of the house with the other chickens, but he found a way through to the bedroom and jumped on the windowsill to be next to us, looking down curiously. He spent the night here, and seemed to be looking forward to coming with us up more mountains.

We'd figured out a new route, crossing first to the other side of the mountain range and stopping at a few villages along the way, and I was excited and ready to go. Suzanna had injured her leg and spoke of leaving but I motivated her to try it first. The others gradually began to get motivated too.

Luckily the rain stopped and we left with heavy bags, full of food for the next two weeks. It was only 6km to the next village but the rain had destroyed the paths so it was paddy fields, rivers and mud all over again. At the village, we learned that it was forbidden to climb the mountain pass we were heading for on a Tuesday – of course – so we waited it out and got a big room complete with a couple of big spiders. The local people piled into the room to watch us eat, then Liva kept us awake by coughing and snoring like a madman.

The next morning was sunny, luckily, but our path took us again across rivers and thick mud. Up the mountain path we climbed and slid back and fell, over and over. It was ruined from the rain and the zebu that tramped it. Suzanna cursed in at least five languages. I got stuck in the mud and my sandal broke again, so I switched to trainers.

Finally we made it out of the jungle to more open mountains. On the mountain passes it was beautiful but we had to stay focused, as the cliffs were steep and dangerous in places. We followed these paths for a few days. At a tiny village we stopped to cook noodles but I managed to burn myself and spilt half my bowl on the floor. Gertrude ate it for me, then the other chickens started to gather. Gertrude chased them off and attacked one of the others. I knew he'd won three cock-fights previously, so I held him back and broke it up.

The villagers were busy crushing rice and doing other chores when we woke up early to a hot sun and blue sky. My appetite had gone, but I forced some food down. We climbed to a small village and the heat was intense. We took river breaks so Gertrude could drink water and cool down. I was finding it tough and had zero energy. I wondered if I should have tackled the island the other way around, from north to south, in order to have more strength to tackle these mountains.

Four hours later we hit the village of Anpany, seemingly in the middle of nowhere, where locals told us they believed it was impossible to summit the mountain we were heading for, Sambirano. They knew of a guide, the "mountain man", a 50-year-old man as fit as a fiddle who knew the mountains better than anyone there. He was currently working out in the paddy field. So we decided to wait and stay the night; they had just killed a pig so we looked forward to some meaty food that evening – Liva especially got very excited about it. I had a wash at the river, saw a snake eat a frog, washed my socks and relaxed outside our hut listening to music, while Liva went to search for the man.

I had noticed two lumps on my arm, white with raw red around – some kind of infection? We now looked more closely and could see holes pierced in the skin. The locals said it looked like spider bites. The lumps blistered up and filled with pus, so I had to keep them covered up. The peak of Sambirano wasn't too far away now but we knew it was going to be difficult. Max looked worried and frustrated, and that rubbed off on me. We watched the rain come crashing down, knowing this was the wrong time to be in the mountains. In the rainy season between November and April, Madagascar regularly gets hammered by big tropical cyclones bringing dangerous storms, violent winds and heavy winds that can flood large areas and cause mudslides, causing deaths and injuries among the local population.

The mountain man, called Lemaro, arrived early the next morning and said he'd never been to the summit of Sambirano and didn't know anyone else who had. He was the guide that Gilles used when taking people to Maromokotro via this village, but he'd never been asked to go to the summit of Sambirano in all his 50 years – he didn't think even his parents had ever done it.

It was awful news to hear. However, he did know the way up. He didn't want to take us to the summit as he thought it was just a cliff face and he also worried about coming back down alone; the rivers were strong now and we needed to work as a team to get across them. But he could join us for long enough to show us the way up the peak, and point us in the right direction.

We thought about it, and decided to leave Suzanna and Liva behind in case something went wrong, and just Max and I would take on the mountain – travelling lighter as we could leave unnecessary kit with them. We had a big breakfast and set out, hoping to reach the summit that afternoon – Lemaro said it was possible from here – and make it back in one day. We were ready and determined to get it done. At first he took his time, stopping to chat to people, which made me think it must be close. Then we set out on the same old routine of river crossings, steep climbs, slippery paths. Clouds covered the peaks and the rain came down, and we began hacking our path through the jungle. We'd been walking all day when Lemaro suddenly stopped and spoke to Max.

"Here it is."

Andohanisambirano means "source of the mountain". The guide thought we wanted to get to the water source, not the summit. All that time with Max and Liva explaining – and we'd ended up at the wrong place. Max tried to justify it but he knew what the mission was. I was gobsmacked and we had a bit of an argument. We could see the mountain we needed to climb, but the peak was covered in cloud and mist. I tried the GPS but couldn't find it as it wasn't labelled; GPS tends to be useless with this type of thing, it's much better to use a map and compass. Lemaro said he would stay and help us to the summit, which was good of him, as he knew the forest better than anyone and knew there was a huge risk of our getting lost.

We found a small track but it was late afternoon and would be getting dark soon, so we walked to lower ground and found a flat place to sleep, clearing the bamboo and using the stalks as poles to hang a shelter from, and vines to tie it down. We put out our bowls to collect the rainwater running down the shelter, since there was no water, and made a bamboo stand for the pots. A swift bit of bushcraft. Lemaro had caught a small mammal called a tenrec and cooked that with the rice and noodles. I spent a while trying to match the mountain from the map to the GPS, eventually succeeding, and yes, we were looking at the correct mountain, Andohanisambirano: at 2,501 metres, the fifth highest in Madagascar. It was two and a half miles away, so we were hoping for a clear view of it the next morning.

And there it was: I had a perfect match on my GPS, we had our mountain, and we just needed to summit it. Easier said than done – but now our guide was an experienced, hard-core bushman who knew the jungle like a park. We decided to leave the shelter up and the rucksack under it so we could move faster. There were barely any tracks, mainly just animal tracks. We were hacking most of the time, crawling, climbing, trying to get through. We sustained a lot of cuts. There was a thorny creeper that wrapped itself around us and razor-sharp bamboo shards sticking out of the ground, and a strong plant that tripped us up. It was lethal. In four hours we covered half a mile and I started to worry.

Suddenly, as we emerged from the jungle to a clearing with a lake, Lemaro turned and gestured to us to be quiet, then approach softly. He pointed towards the ducks on the water. They had bright white eyes that stood out from their brown plumage, and there were a family or two with ducklings swimming together. When they sensed our presence they flew off, and Lemaro explained they were pochard ducks, only found right here and in Ranomafana – in fact, the rarest duck in the world. He had heard about this all his life but had never seen it before, and seemed pleased.

Then we were back to crawling, climbing and hacking through vegetation. It was energy draining and sometimes painful, but we were getting close. Max left his wet shirt behind and we went for it. And finally, we made it to the summit, enclosed by thick jungle. It was amazing to be in such untouched wilderness.

I sent a quick message to the world, did a recording then we headed straight back down. We had a long way back down and clouds came in to block the view and bring heavy rain. We made it to the shelter at 6pm and got a fire started. I had no dry top and was in for a cold night, so slept with my head next to the fire. We were hungry but in high spirits, cold and wet with cuts and leeches all over our bodies, laughing and shivering, almost touching the fire to get some warmth. We had summited the dreaded mountain.

When we made it back to the others the next day, I found out a local had stolen my trousers, so I wouldn't have a dry pair to change into and would have to wear the same wet pair all the time. I helped out making sugar cane tea – big effort for little reward. There were no luxuries or comforts here – it was rice for every meal. We managed to get an omelette to share between four of us to go with the rice. The only alternative was manioc, which was like plain porridge. We talked a lot amongst ourselves of how easy it is in the Western world to make a cup of tea or get some food, and how different it was out here.

The next goal was the plateau for Maromokotro, the eighth and final mountain. The locals warned us about two big rivers. The first wasn't too deep but the current was strong and we worked as a team to help each other across, balancing the bags on our heads. Lemurs swarmed our camp one morning. We waved tree branches in front of our faces to battle the tiny flies that constantly aimed for our eyes, nose, ears and mouth. I started to limp. My trainers had been soaked through for days, and sand inside was rubbing my feet raw. Max said I needed to let my shoes and socks dry out properly by the fire and keep them dry. The next day my feet were slightly better at first, but it wasn't long before they were agony again. I borrowed Liva's flip-flops, three sizes too big, to summit the beautiful mountain of Maromokotro which now appeared before us.

We ditched the bags on the side of the mountain and placed a waterproof cover over them for the last section, taking just my sat phone, Gertrude, the rum and honey. We were all soaked through fairly quickly and the walk seemed to go on for ever. We had estimated two hours but it took four, as the path had grown over and the lads were slightly lost. Suzanna had a nasty fall walking over some rocks.

I had Gertrude in my arms and when it started raining, he tried escaping as he hated it; I had to grip tight and keep hold of him until the summit. When we eventually made it, we were freezing so we had no reason to linger. We quickly freed poor old Gertrude, who was freezing also, and hid in the rocks away from the rain. We had some rum and honey. I tried to send a message off to the world but my hands were too wet to work the phone.

"Well, we've got to the summit," I said. "Let's head back down."

I wanted so much to get off that cold, rainy mountain, but it wasn't easy. The rain and wind were horrendous, we were dripping, there were now rivers forming and lightning strikes right above us, and we were lost all day long. Max couldn't find the path off the mountain, and we walked back and forth constantly, looking for the river that he knew. It was a killer. We found a river but Max said it wasn't the one. The rain picked up more and we were forced to hack wood and assemble a shelter on the mountain, feeling very vulnerable. It was horrible, nerve-wracking.

Eventually the weather cleared. We climbed a hill which provided views and Max could now see where we needed to be.

We worked our way down a tricky traverse over rough terrain and after an hour or so, we made it to a river. There was some Malagasy talk between Liva and Max, and I thought something was wrong. Max went on ahead and when we caught up, Suzanna asked him:

"Is this the right river – do you recognise it?"

"No," he said.

I was gutted and threw down my bag.

"Only joking!" he said.

I think we all cheered.

When we finally set up camp, I pulled the tape from my foot and the skin came with it, which hurt. But it was done: I had successfully summited the eight highest mountains in Madagascar, and it felt bloody good.

We still had to get to the tip of the island, of course.

The next big river was too deep and the current was too strong for us to cross it on foot. Max had already lost his shoe on the last crossing. We realised we'd have to build a raft. So we gathered materials from the bush. It took hours, but we managed to tie together bamboo trunks using a long grass as string. We put two bags on it and Liva swam across, carrying a string we'd made by tying together the guy ropes from the tents. He held it at the other side of the river, and we attached the raft to it, and went across one by one. The rivers were now scarily powerful and it was clear we shouldn't be there in this season. That crossing took so long that we just had to eat mangoes and press on. I was glad we had Liva with us. He was always positive and optimistic. Whenever we were scrambling in the rain to put up a shelter, he'd be there whistling away. Sometimes I'd catch him unawares and see things were getting to him, but if he saw me looking at him he'd put a big brave smile on.

At the next village, just a handful of huts, Max knew some of the guys and they gave us meat and rice, which tasted delicious. They said we'd have to take a different route from the one Max knew, as it was too difficult in the rainy season. I suggested we pay for one of them to come with us just to get us there without getting lost or taking the wrong route. They went behind the huts to discuss it. At first they said no; then one guy said he could do it but needed to be back tomorrow morning, so he'd have to take us that night. We'd be walking in the dark on difficult paths, but we loved the sound of this and decided to go for it.

He led us at a fast pace over hills, bog land and more in the pouring rain. Sand gathered in my flip flops and socks, which were three sizes too big – this was painful and slowing me down. Night fell as we were on the mountain top. I got my head torch out which was low on battery. I was slipping and tripping all over the place. We finally made it to the main river, the Mahavavy.

The guy went across first to drop off his stuff. It was raining slightly, pitch black and the current was crazy strong. We had to form a strong chain, link up and hold hands, then work our way across. We all held hands and started to cross, but then we hit the most powerful section, in which we had to climb up on to a submerged rock; it meant the river would then be up to our waists instead of our chests. The guide went first, then Max with great difficulty, then Suzanna attempted but slipped. Max and I were holding her on either side as she tried to get her footing. She was facing the wrong way and I shouted over the roaring of the river that she had to turn around. It meant I had to let go of her arm, so I waited to be sure Max had her to keep the river from pulling her down, and when she had some grip, then I let her go. They were all struggling: one slip and they were all down with the current in the pitch black. She screamed, but the lads at last pulled her onto the rock.

Once Suzanna saw the other side and was able to make it, she bolted for safety, injuring Max accidentally in her haste by twisting him into a rock because they were all still linked. But they made it, leaving just me and Liva. The guide then came back for us, and we held hands and attempted our crossing again. Our bags were big and as soon as we hit the current it pushed us so hard and almost took the bags. We were now on our tip toes and in my oversized flip flops I couldn't grip the rock properly. I slipped and was up to my chin, dangling, gripping with all my strength onto the guy's hand. But I couldn't grip the rock and our grip on each other was loosening. I kicked off my flip flops and just as I gripped the rock with one of my knees, Liva lost his footing.

The guy now had both our weights and the bags, all being dragged by the current. I was pretty sure that was it. Liva shouted to us to let him go otherwise we'd all go, but somehow we managed to squeeze hard and keep hold of each other's hands. I heard Suzanna scream again. I managed to get one foot on the rock and pull Liva up too. We were all on the rock and now needed to make our way across to safety.

It was a close call and I still don't know how we made it. Suzanna was crying. I was now buzzed up, full of adrenaline, screaming, "WHOOOOO!!" It had been terrifying.

Madagascar was throwing everything at us.

Would we actually make it? From being stuck on mountains to blocked by high rivers… It was frustrating and exhausting.

We eventually approached Ambilobe, and just as we joined the national road, my sandal broke again. We walked on. I was soaked with one sandal on and one in my hand, pants hanging off me. Max had bare feet. Suzanna was limping. We were a mess. It had been a lot tougher than I expected, but after a couple of close calls, such as the scary moment we had experienced in the river, we'd all made it out alive.

As we eased back into civilisation and rewarded ourselves with pizza, chips, bruschetta, prawn cocktail and pancakes with chocolate, we looked back over the past days. We had come through life-threatening situations, Suzanna especially in the river. That had been terrifying – for me, as well as for her, because I felt responsible. It didn't bear thinking about what would have happened if we'd lost our grip. It was the toughest thing she had ever done, she said, laughing nervously. She was tough and had overcome a lot.

I was over the moon that we had all made it down off the mountains safely.

On day 146, I woke up and jumped straight in the shower, excited to start out. I had no worries for the next four days: just an easy tarmac road which would take us straight to our destination of Diego, the northernmost city of Madagascar, close to the northern tip. Before we left, I searched for sun cream and socks, which I couldn't find anywhere, but I had plenty of ice cream while looking.

Suzanna and Liva were packing, getting ready to go back to Antananarivo. I hugged Suzanna, told her to stay in touch and have a safe trip back. She wished me and Max luck for the final section. I thanked Liva for being part of the team. I couldn't have asked for someone better to join us for that section – he was a true warrior and I appreciated that. We all hugged one another and waved goodbye, hoping to see one another again in the big city.

It was a straightforward, plain-sailing walk to Diego, also known as Antsiranana. On the last day it threw it down with rain, but Max and I were in our element and I felt a big buzz of excitement about the end of the journey. I wanted to keep going, but I had an invitation to visit the last of the conservation areas to look for the northern sportive lemur, one of the world's rarest primates.

It was still raining, cyclone season. At Diego we were picked up by a 4x4 to go to the national park but it broke down in deep mud. A lorry full of guys helped to push us out, but we broke down again so had to ditch the vehicle and walk. We finally made it, though. The conservationists were increasing the numbers of this critically endangered species; they were educating the locals and providing them with areas where they could take the trees, and continue with the planting, so they wouldn't destroy the forest that was the lemurs' natural habitat. There was a lot of good being done, and I was lucky to spot one of those small, agile creatures with their big brown eyes. It seemed a fitting end to my Madagascar experience.

Then we just had the final walk to Cap D'Ambre, which should only take two days. The northern tip of Madagascar is like an arrowhead sticking out from the rest of the island so we had to take a boat over a small strip of water. We set out with two young locals who said they'd trek with us for a small fee as they'd been there before; we just wanted to get to the finish and it was great to know we'd find the route.

Those two days of walking and camping were absolute hell. The paths were pure mud and swampland. I broke my sandals after the first one or two hours so had to borrow a too-small pair of trainers from one of the lads, which were quite old and the soles worn thin. We were drenched and cold and made very slow progress, sinking in the mud. I was all geared up to get to the end, but there was still a hard push to go.

When the end came after 155 days, at the wild, empty point of Cap D'Ambre with its lighthouse looking out over the deep blue waves, I wish I could say it felt amazing but it just felt well overdue. After all those near misses, all I can say is that I was chuffed to arrive in one piece. I'd avoided the dangerous bandits in the south, the malaria hadn't stopped me and I'd made it over the mountain range and raging rivers alive. I was relieved.

There was no glamorous ending with people there to meet us and crack a bottle of Champagne; none of that. Max was against drinking and anyway there was no one around even if we'd wanted to. We cheered – and got ready for the two-day walk back the way we'd come.

But when we got back to Diego, I could finally put my bag down, knowing I wouldn't have to pick it up again for a while. We had a banana shake each. I was very, very glad to be done.

# EPILOGUE: Pushing on

I had no idea what would come my way once completing my expeditions, but that's the beauty of taking on a risky adventure. If I'd failed, at least I'd have tried. Succeeding as I did brought many opportunities my way. I have had so many, simply as a result of taking the plunge and giving it a go.

Putting in the hard work and dedication, correct planning and training were a great recipe to succeed. Of course making it back in one piece helps, but once arriving home - this saw me taking on a whole new adventure.

Completion of both my world first expeditions resulted in a lot of media interest. I found myself on the TV, in Newspapers and many magazine articles. This great publicity was a catalyst for my career in the adventure world and added much credibility to my endeavours especially when searching out sponsors.

I have been fortunate enough to be invited to give talks in many Schools and Corporate companies, not just here in the uk but overseas also. I guess this is the byproduct of what i love doing. To explore places untouched by others, soak up the cultures and diversity and to also push myself in extreme situations. This is who I am and I feel like I am only just getting started.

Learning at the age of 16 to make a mindmap was indeed invaluable. Breaking every goal down into steps I needed to take always stuck with me. Even helping me out in later years, saving my life in the Gobi Desert. Whatever my goal, I always make myself a list of what I need to do, what I need to target first, section by section. It helps me plan. My life is full of lists.

I find the planning of my expeditions very exciting. Enthusiasm and passion for my chosen destinations flows in the early stages and I cannot wait to get started.

These countries I have traversed have their difficulties like many others do, but I found it a natural progression to highlight their hardships during my journey. Teaming up with The Lemur Conservation Network in Madagascar was a huge honour, as the work they do is invaluable. Raising awareness along with Malaria No More UK on the devastating effects of this disease has also been a profound learning curve, especially experiencing it at first-hand myself, I am in awe of the hard work and dedication sustained by this organisation.

My confidence has grown through my travels and adventures and I draw on my own resilience and determination. But I am always listening and learning from others I meet along my journey. I suppose the first people I learnt from were of course my parents, and my dad in particular helped me enormously in the early planning stages, and his guidance and advice were invaluable. They were and are always supportive of what I choose to do, and that mattered, and helped a huge amount. It also helped that they said I'd have to work hard and save the money I needed in order to make my goals/dreams happen. It was an important lesson that I would have to learn to do things for myself and be self-driven and motivated. Whatever you want to do, the opportunities are there and it's up to you to explore them. It really doesn't matter if no one else sees it for you; it's important that you see it for yourself! I hope in some way the stories that I have shared help to motivate and inspire your own journey through life.

The world's a big place and I'd urge you go to places you've never been and do things you've never done. As it's this that gets your heart beating – and when your heart's beating, man, you're truly living .......

# ACKNOWLEDGEMENTS

I'd like to thank my parents first and foremost, for their guidance and showing so much support, for believing in me and for all those sleepless nights I caused them.

My family, friends and all supporters, who always back me and provide messages of encouragement; there is nothing more humbling and motivating than to be able to share my experiences with everyone and for it to be received with such positivity.

My logistics managers Rob Mills and Gilles Gautier at Madamax for providing expert knowledge and services to help make these expeditions possible.

Jenya and Ogi at Blackshaman who helped with logistics in Mongolia, and Manantena at Madamax who did so in Madagascar. Such focus and drive to help make sure the expeditions stayed on track, for which I am so grateful.

My three guides throughout Madagascar – Max, Mi and Joe for helping to make the expedition achievable, such solid guys who stood by my side in the face of adversity, we went through thick and thin with each other, but made it through to the other side even stronger.

I'd also like to thank Jennifer Barclay for her hard work and patience while working on this book with me.

Huge thanks to my backers and supporters:-

Craghoppers
Ffit Conwy
Felix Gill
Silvergate Plastics
Progress School of Motoring
Edge Transport
Burbidge's Bakery
Pioneer Expeditions
Haglofs
Hench Nutrition
Lemur Network Conservation
Maui Jim
Suzanna Tierie
Paul Woosey
Jen Barclay
Sean Knott, Photography
Mark Lucas, Graphic Design and Art Direction

# About Eye Books

Eye Books is a small independent publisher that passionately believes the more you put into life the more you get out of it.

It publishes stories that show ordinary people can and do achieve extraordinary things.

Its books celebrate "living" rather than merely existing.

It is committed to ethical publishing and tries to minimise its carbon footprint in the manufacturing and distribution of its books.

**www.eye-books.com**

About Extraordinary Things Done by Ordinary People